SCIENCE

A.S.A.P*

*As Soon As Possible,
As Simple As Possible

Alan Axelrod, Ph.D.

Prentice
Hall Press

For Anita and Ian

Prentice Hall Press
Published by The Berkley Publishing Group
A member of Penguin Group (USA) Inc.
375 Hudson Street
New York, New York 10014

Copyright © 2003 by Alan Axelrod
Text design by Tiffany Kukec
Cover design by Ben Gibson
Cover photo by Ryoichi Utsumi/Photonica
Additional photo copyright © by Dennis Kunkel Microscopi, Inc.

Prentice Hall Press edition: August 2003

This book has been catalogued by the Library of Congress

Printed in the United States of America

10   9   8   7   6   5   4   3   2   1

Contents

MEDIEVAL SCIENCE

RENAISSANCE SCIENCE

ENLIGHTENMENT SCIENCE

PRELUDE TO MODERN SCIENCE

THE ATOM AND THE AIRPLANE

OUTER SPACE, INNER SPACE, AND CYBERSPACE

MODERN SCIENCE

What This Is and What This Isn't

Science A.S.A.P. has been written as an informal, very readable, and highly efficient one-stop source for all the science the general reader needs in order to stake a legitimate claim to cultural literacy. The book is not a compact review of scientific principles, nor is it a brief encyclopedia. Instead, it looks at science historically, highlighting key discoveries, inventions, and theoretical formulations everyone needs to know about, and it uses them as sturdy springboards to related discoveries, inventions, and theories and, even more important, to the ideas, concepts, and themes that underlie and inform the scientific approach to reality. Counting the main entries as well as the sidebars within some of those entries, there are only 202 items here, but they are leveraged into a full-scale appreciation of the movement of science from 500,000 B.C. through 2003—the year this book was completed.

ANCIENT
SCIENCE

Homo Erectus Tames Fire

The first hard archaeological evidence of the purposeful use of fire is found in a cave near Beijing, China. Here, along with remains of *Homo erectus*—a hominid, precursor of today's human beings (*Homo sapiens*), who lived between one million and three million B.C.—are traces of campfires.

The controlled use of fire—starting, perpetuating, applying, and stopping it—is not only essential to the activities of human society; it is also a basic skill that sets human beings apart from other animals. No wonder the ancient Greeks thought of fire as the divine gift to humanity, conveyed by Prometheus. Fire provides us with light that defies the night, with heat that defies the climate, with a weapon against stronger animals, and with a means to cook their meat—to render otherwise unpalatable, even inedible, foods useful. Fire also opened the way to myriad processes of transforming raw materials into useful objects. Its "discovery" by *Homo erectus* was the foundation of all technology.

Agriculture and Irrigation Develop in Northern Iraq

Before about 8000 B.C., human beings were largely wanderers, their nomadic mode of existence dictated not by some romantic wanderlust, but by the way they got their food: afoot and on the hoof. People were chiefly hunters who followed the migrating herds, though they also gathered whatever wild edibles grew nearby. Even those groups living among nonmigrating animals did not put down roots. Animals that stayed in one place were not, alas, to be had in limitless supply, so when the edible beasts dwindled in one location, it was time to move on to another.

The paramount feature of nomadic life is impermanence. Nomads do not build; their energies are directed toward moving, hunting, and moving again. There is no impetus or incentive to invest in, to improve, or to enhance any particular place.

Based on archaeological evidence, it is apparent that a new mode of living appeared around 8000 B.C. People began purposely planting seeds, watching them grow, watering them, then harvesting the results. No one has any idea how—or even why—this invention, agriculture, came about, but it did. And it gave groups of people a reason to stay in one place, especially when animal herding was added to agriculture. No longer did the source of food have to be ceaselessly pursued. Like the plants they cultivated, people began to put down roots.

The idea that food could be actively produced rather than passively followed was a great advance in what we think of as civilization: the creation of continuous, cohesive settlements and cultures.

Settlement called for building—not just shelters, but structures of all kinds, including structures of the intellect: ideas and systems. For now there was time to sit and think and formulate and invent. As great a step as agriculture was, there was still much that lay beyond the human capacity to control. One could plant a seed, but if a steady supply of water were not present, the seed would not become food. If human beings were no longer shackled to migrating herds, they were still the helpless vassals of rain and the victims of drought.

Archaeological evidence that people began to cultivate and harvest water as they had earlier begun to cultivate and harvest crops appears about 5000 B.C. Rain falls on land as well as on bodies of water. Rivers run with water long after a rain shower ceases. By about 5000 B.C., people began to dig ditches from the riverbanks into the land nearby. In this way, more land became productive more dependably and for longer periods. Of course, this required work—and not just a one-time commitment to dig ditches. The water flowing through them wore the ditches away, brought silt, caused them to collapse. Irrigation ditches required continual maintenance. Cooperation, collaboration, coordination were called for, and this required leadership, the rudiments of social structure, law, and government. If agriculture gave people a reason to stay put and the means to do so, irrigation provided a motive for the creation of what we call the city-state, the forerunner of nations.

Copper, Bronze, and Iron Come into Use

Archaeologists believe that hominids, the precursors of current human beings, learned how to use tools and weapons long before they learned to use fire—although the use of fire certainly enabled the creation of more and better tools and weapons. Stone, bone, and wood were the readily available materials from which the tools were fashioned, and since stone is by far the most durable, it is the stone tools that archaeologists have found in greatest abundance, and the period in which human beings used stone tools is generally called the Stone Age.

Over the centuries, early makers and users of stone tools must have devoted a great deal of time to searching out stones, and some that they found were unusual, heavy, shiny, and malleable—that is, when struck, they did not split or shatter, but dented and spread. These were metals, albeit the relatively rare metals that, chemically inert, do not combine with other substances readily. Most metal ore is exclusively found combined with nonmetallic stuff in rocks and so just looks like more rock. But relatively inert metals such as silver, gold, and copper are sometimes found in a free state, as pure metal nuggets.

By 5000 B.C., people were trading nuggets and even beating them into ornaments—they were too small to do much else with—but within a thousand years, people began separating metal from nonmetallic ore. Copper was the first. When copper ore is heated over a hot wood fire, the carbon liberated from the burning wood combines with the oxygen in the ore and forms carbon dioxide, which escapes to leave behind not a conglomerate of metal and nonmetal, but pure copper.

How was something so momentous discovered? No one knows. We can only assume that various people at various times during this period either built wood fires atop copper ore and noticed the result or perhaps deliberately experimented to see what would happen if certain rocks were thrown into a very hot fire.

Separation of copper from copper ore was an important advance in the science of metallurgy, and it allowed for the increased production of copper ornaments, which, in turn, fostered the wider development of trade among peoples. However, copper was not very practical for making tools. Soft, copper is easily bent and blunted. But those who spent a lot of time extracting copper from ore must have noticed that *some* copper comes out harder than other copper. Why? Because the hard copper is not pure copper, but a combination of copper and tin, which, when smelted from the mixed ore, produces an alloy of the two metals, bronze.

In contrast to copper, bronze is hard. Whereas a copper tool quickly became dull, a bronze tool held its edge. Soon, metalworkers did not rely on the chance finding of mixed copper and tin ores to produce bronze, but purposely smelted the two metals together, creating the bronze alloy at will and giving rise to the so-called Bronze Age, characterized by the production and use of vast quantities of bronze tools, armor, and edged weapons.

Bronze held sway as literally the cutting-edge material of civilization for some two thousand years, from about 3000 to 1000 B.C. During this period—and, doubtless, even earlier—people knew of another metal, even harder and heavier than bronze. They knew it from occasional rocks that fell from the sky, iron meteorites, the only rocks in which iron occurs free from nonmetallic substances. Meteors are extremely rare, and the iron ones must have been prized as precious, because the metal made a supremely strong tool—or weapon.

Before 1000 B.C., metalworkers had obtained copper, gold, silver, bronze, lead, and tin from ore, simply by using very hot wood fires. But a wood fire was not sufficient to free iron trapped in ore.

How to make fire hotter?

If wood is burned in the presence of relatively little oxygen, it produces charcoal—carbon—which, in turn, burns without flame, but at temperatures much greater than those of burning wood. By about 1500 B.C., the Hittite people of Asia Minor produced charcoal and, using it, they were able to smelt iron from ore. But it was never as good as that rare meteoric stuff (which, it turns out, is actually an alloy of iron and nickel); it simply wasn't as hard as a good piece of bronze. It took several hundred more years to discover that if the iron ore was smelted so that some of the resulting iron combined with the carbon in the charcoal, the resulting metal was very hard indeed. In fact, the carbonized iron was steel. By 1000 B.C., this metal was being turned out in great quantity, and the Bronze Age yielded to the Iron Age.

Egyptians Invent the Sundial and the "Modern" Calendar

The measurement of the most abstract of quantities, time, was a great advance in civilization. With it came the capacity to coordinate the actions of many individuals and, therefore, the ability to direct, manage, and govern complex enterprises and societies.

To be sure, human beings must have "told time" since early prehistory, simply by noting the passage of days, the changes of season, and almost certainly, early on, the phases of the moon. Most likely, they also divided the day into some sort of segments based on the position of the sun. But it was not until the appearance of the sundial, apparently in Egypt and probably about 4000 B.C., that any degree of accuracy in the division of the day was achieved. It is known that the Egyptians made extensive use of sundials—little wonder in a sunny climate and location—and that they divided the day into twelve equal parts, named hours.

The systematic measurement of time in the longer term seems to have originated about 2800 B.C. among the peoples of the "fertile crescent," the region watered by the Tigris and Euphrates. However, it was the Egyptians, shortly after this period, who developed a calendar that seems more familiar to us—although it was based on a more local phenomenon than the moon. By careful observation, Egyptian priests discovered that the Nile flooded every 365 days, which coincided with the time it took the sun to make what appeared to be its circuit of the heavens relative to the stars. Using these two coincidental cycles, the Egyptians developed a solar calendar. Returning to the lunar cycles, they divided the year into twelve months, making each month exactly 30 days long—without trying to synchronize the months with the actual phases of the moon. The result was a calendar year of 360 days, to which the Egyptians appended 5 more days at the end, so that the year would reflect the workings of river and sun. The Egyptian calendar was much simpler than anything that had come before, which made it that much more flexible and useful for measuring time across the long term and for planning the future.

The First Calendar, About 2800 B.C.

By about 2800 B.C., the people of the lands adjacent to the Tigris and Euphrates created a calendar—the first of which we have archaeological evidence—that attempts to reconcile the variations in the cycles of the moon with a consistent method of marking the passage of seasonal time. It takes twenty-nine or thirty days for the moon to go through all of its phases, and the cycle of the seasons consumes twelve or thirteen of these cycles. The Tigris-Euphrates calendar was projected over a cycle of nineteen years, during which some years had twelve and others thirteen lunar months. By this means, the lunar calendar meshed with the seasons.

Sumerians and Babylonians Create Mathematics and Astronomy

Who knows when human beings first began to count and to manipulate quantities? It is impossible to say. But the earliest known civilization that went beyond counting and quantities to develop a genuine system of numbers was that of the Sumerians, the people centered in what is today southern Iraq.

By 1800 B.C., they had developed a number system based not on the familiar ten, but on sixty. It is a most intriguing number on which to base a number system. Sixty is easy to manipulate, in that it is readily divisible by many numbers, even and odd: two, three, four, five, six, ten, twelve, fifteen, and thirty. This is ideal for a people heavily engaged in trade and commerce. But the choice of sixty likely went beyond mere convenience, and it is almost certainly no coincidence that, as the Sumerian number system is the earliest of which we have a record, so the immediate successors of the Sumerians, the Babylonians, are remembered as the world's first astronomers. Consider: There are six-times-60 degrees in a circle—360—which very nearly duplicates the apparent movement of the sun around the sky: about 1 degree per day, or 365 degrees per year, which is very close to the 360 degrees of a circle.

From virtually the earliest *recorded* times, then, mathematics and astronomy were joined. Numbers were very useful for counting cattle, people, and goods, but, thousands of years ago, those who watched the skies discerned a deeper significance in numbers. They felt a higher connection, between numbers and the motions of what they saw in the heavens. In the simultaneous formulation of mathematics and astronomical observation by the peoples of the great valley of the Tigris and the Euphrates we have the first evidence of what we today call science: the postulation of theory, the discernment of system and meaning in the world, a connection between mind and universe, a passion to look beyond the visible and the apparent for an explanation of all that is visible and apparent.

The Invention of Writing, About 3500 B.C.

The Sumerians produced writing long before they created mathematics. By 3500 B.C., a pressing need to track grain production and trade prompted the Sumerians to create unique symbols to stand for certain numbers and certain items, such as *grain, cow, human being,* and so on. The earliest symbols were, in effect, crude drawings of the objects represented. These evolved into standardized wedge-shaped indentations made with a stylus in a soft clay tablet: *cuneiform,* from the Greek for "wedge-shaped," writing.

Since the eighteenth century, when it was first described, cuneiform has been assumed to be the oldest surviving writing. However, in April 2003, archaeologists announced the results of preliminary analysis of symbols carved into eight, 600-year-old tortoise shells found in twenty-four Neolithic graves at Jiahu in Henan province, western China. It is quite possible that these signs, thousands of years older than cuneiform, will prove to be the earliest examples of writing, although it will require a good deal of study to determine if the symbols really belong to a genuine writing system.

Thales Conceptualizes the Elements

Great science has always asked the big questions, and few questions are bigger than "What is the universe made of?" Certainly, thoughtful people asked this question before 580 B.C., but the answers they came up with were based on myth, tradition, or faith rather than reasoning built on observation. When the Greek philosopher Thales asked the question in 580 B.C., he did not base his answer on religion, legend, or folk wisdom, but on observation, which he used to formulate a theory.

In itself, this was a great advance in science, whose very core is rational inquiry. As for the theory Thales formulated, well, it was, on the face of it, wrong! He concluded that all matter was water, either in the familiar form of liquid water or water in a transformed or altered state. Today, of course, no scientist believes that everything is made of water, but look deeper into Thales's theory and it is apparent that he conceptualized a cornerstone of modern physics and chemistry: the idea of elements as the building blocks of all matter. Wrong in the details, Thales was quite right in the concept.

500 B.C.

Alcmaeon Performs the First Recorded Human Dissection

Science is about rational inquiry, yet it is also driven by a powerful human passion, for which the word *curiosity* seems pale, weak, and inadequate. Driven by the passion of their curiosity, many scientists have defied religious dogma and social convention. One such was Alcmaeon, who, about 500 B.C., became the first physician (of whom we have record) to dissect a human corpse—in bold defiance of Greek religious scruples and traditions. Alcmaeon was able to differentiate between veins and arteries, and he observed that the organs of sensation were linked to the brain by nerves. Beyond this, he did not leave any detailed anatomical studies, but his action broke new ground by elevating firsthand observation to the status of a scientific necessity above all other considerations.

440 B.C.

Democritus Proposes the Atom as the Smallest Particle of Matter

I n 440 B.C., the Greek philosopher Democritus took the idea of the element, as advanced by Thales (see "580 B.C.: Thales Conceptualizes the Elements"), much further by theorizing that all matter consists of tiny particles, too tiny to see and so small that nothing smaller was possible. With the keen logic of the Greek philosophical tradition, Democritus reasoned that if a particle were the smallest particle possible, it was by definition indivisible. This got to the true nature of an *element* as the basic, irreducible substance of matter. Democritus called such particles *atoms,* from a Greek word signifying indivisibility.

Unlike Thales's water theory, the atomic theory of Democritus was not based on observation, but speculation. This, too, is permitted in science, but such reasoning is never complete without experimental—observational—proof. In the case of atoms, that would not come for some two thousand years. During the long period of Western history known as the Dark Ages, roughly A.D. 476 to 1000, and far into the Middle Ages, the brilliance of Thales, Democritus, and most of the other philosophers of classical Greece would be forgotten, or even surprised.

Euclid Creates the Elements of Geometry

Zoser, first king of Egypt's Third Dynasty, came to power in 2650 B.C., whereupon construction was begun on a massive "step pyramid," about 200 feet high and on a base of approximately 400 feet by 350 feet. It was the first of the pyramids and, perhaps, the first large stone structure ever built. Today, it remains as the earliest large-scale human structure in existence. From it, we can only infer that the Egyptians, at least as early as 2650 B.C., had developed considerable knowledge of geometry, at least on a practical, journeyman level. It was not until millennia later, however, about 300 B.C., that the Greek mathematician Euclid lifted geometry from the realm of the builder and artisan to that of the philosopher. In a book he titled *Elements,* Euclid compiled and synthesized all that was known of geometry at the time.

Analyzing a vast body of geometrical observation, Euclid developed a handful of axioms, a foundation of principles whose self-evidence required no proof. Building on these, Euclid constructed a series of theorems, the proofs of which depended on the axioms and on theorems previously proved.

Euclid's achievement in *Elements* has, of course, contributed mightily to the human-built world, but his contribution to thought and the intellectual process is even more profound. For Euclid removed from the physical world such tangibles as points, lines, curves, planes, and solids, and imported them into the realm of the mind. He did what countless scientists have done and continue to do daily: modeled reality in the imagination, where it can be examined, manipulated, and extended in myriad ways impossible or impractical in the physical world.

The Abacus, About 500 B.C.

Euclid's genius was in elevating the physical world to the realm of abstract idea. However, physical calculation—arithmetic—remained an important aspect of mathematics long after Euclid. The ancient computer known as the abacus may well have existed before 500 B.C., when it is known that Egyptians were using it, but the earliest archaeological evidence dates from this time. The abacus is an elegantly simple means of manipulating numbers by exploiting the base of a particular number system. Beads are strung on a series of wires suspended in a frame. In a base 10 system (the decimal system we are familiar with), ten beads are strung on each wire. The beads of the first wire represent ones, those of the second, tens, those of the third, hundreds, and so on. With practice, the basic arithmetical operations can be performed quickly.

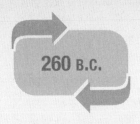

260 B.C.

Archimedes Articulates the Principle of the Lever

As with the wheel and axle, the inclined plane, and other simple machines, the inventor of the lever is unknown. Doubtless, there was no single inventor, in any case, just practical people who, at various times, used a stick to pry up a rock or other heavy object, then, intuitively, figured out that it made even more sense to put a rock or other object (we call this a fulcrum) under the pry stick, and press down rather than pull up.

Intuitive, practical engagement with the world around us is a wonderful and highly useful thing, but it is hit or miss, and it holds little hope for any significant technological progress. How far would technical civilization progress if each individual had to discover the lever and fulcrum for himself and on his own, or if he depended on lore or even imitation for his knowledge of this simple machine, not to mention the others?

Scientists neither ignore nor disdain the practical and intuitive, but, for them, these things are never enough. Their urge is to reach behind and beyond the surface of practice and intuition, to develop the principles from which phenomena, actions, and causes and effects flow. This is the creation of theory, and one of the most brilliant theorists of the classical world was Archimedes.

An acute observer of the physical world, Archimedes was even more incisive in his ability to reduce what he observed to precise mathematical description. About 260 B.C., he worked out the mathematics of the lever, providing a theoretical means by which the most mechanically efficient length of lever and placement of fulcrum could be determined based on the weight of the object to be lifted and the height to which one wished to elevate it. Because he had established a complete mathematical theory of levers, Archimedes was able to declare with more than boastful hyperbole, "Give me a lever and a place to stand, and I'll move the world."

Eratosthenes Calculates the Size of the Earth

Virtually all science begins with intense and original observation. Typically, the things others overlook or take for granted are precisely what draw the attention of the scientist. Take Eratosthenes (ca. 276–194 B.C.), who observed that, at the town of Syene (present-day Aswan, Egypt), southeast of Alexandria, the rays of the sun were precisely vertical at noon during the summer solstice. Separately, he observed that, at Alexandria, at exactly the same date and time, the sunlight fell at an angle of 7.5 degrees from the vertical. The difference was small, but Eratosthenes craved an explanation for it, small or not.

Eratosthenes assumed—correctly, as it turns out—that the sun was very far from the earth. This being the case, for all practical purposes, its rays are parallel when they strike the earth. He further believed, as Aristotle had taught, that the earth was a globe. Now, a circle—the flat representation of a globe—contains 360 degrees, and 7.5 degrees (the extent to which sunlight falling on Alexandria at the summer solstice varied from the vertical) is approximately one-fiftieth of 360. Therefore, Eratosthenes concluded, the circumference of the earth must be fifty times the distance between Alexandria and Syene. As measured in Eratosthenes's time, the distance between these two places was 5,000 *stadia,* so he concluded that the circumference of the earth was 250,000 *stadia.* Modern scholars assume that the *stadion* is equivalent to 521.4 feet; therefore, Eratosthenes's calculation of the earth's circumference comes out to 23,990.4 miles and the diameter to 7,578.6

miles. These figures are startlingly close to what we know today as the earth's circumference—24,887.64 miles—and its diameter, 7,926 miles.

Using the apparently meager information available to him, and without instrumentation of any kind, Eratosthenes made a measurement far beyond any physical capacity to do so. It was a triumph of inference.

In addition to measuring the circumference of the earth, Eratosthenes also accurately measured the tilt of the earth's axis, and he compiled an accurate and enormously impressive star catalog. The calendar he formulated was the first to include leap years. For all these reasons, many historians of science consider Eratosthenes the first astronomer in anything approaching the modern sense of the word. That is, he used his senses to make penetrating, remarkable observations precisely in order to move beyond what his mere senses could tell him.

Mapping the Stars, About 350 B.C.

About a century before Eratosthenes calculated the size of the earth, another Greek, Eudoxus, looked to the stars. About 350 B.C., this Greek mathematician who had already drawn the best map of the known world up to his time, created the first known star map, inventing, in the process, a system of lines of longitude and latitude to impose order on the apparently random distribution of the stars.

MEDIEVAL
SCIENCE

A.D. 250

Diophantus Writes the First Algebra Text

Geometry dominated Greek mathematical thought through most of the great classical age of Greece, and the development of geometry represented a profound progress from merely managing quantities and shapes to creating theories that allowed the logical and imaginative manipulation of numbers and space. The next step was to integrate numbers and symbols, and the first text that accomplished this was written about A.D. 250 by the Greek mathematician Diophantus. In effect, this is the first known algebra text—although the word *algebra* would not come into existence until much later, when the Persian mathematician Muhammad ibn al-Khwarizmi wrote in 825 a text titled *Hisab al-jabr w'al-musqabalah* (Science of the Reunion and the Opposition). It was this volume that introduced algebra into Europe, and the word *al-jabr,* roughly signifying the transposition of terms from one side of an equation to the other, became Latinized as *algebra.* (See "825: Muhammad ibn al-Khwarizmi Conceptualizes Zero.")

Zosimus Writes the Book on Alchemy

Just as no one knows when, precisely, human beings began to use tools to manipulate and modify their world, it is impossible to say when people began purposefully combining various substances to create new ones. But it was about 300 that an Egyptian named Zosimus wrote a text summing up, systematically, all that was known about chemical change. Because the work of Zosimus combined much mysticism and lore with something approaching practical chemistry, the text is considered the first work of alchemy rather than chemistry. Whereas chemistry is the science of the structure, composition, properties, and reactions of matter, alchemy is a mystical philosophy involving the manipulation of substances and aimed not so much at systematically understanding the nature of matter as at transforming "base metals" (lead and iron, for instance) into gold. Nevertheless, modern chemistry is clearly rooted in ancient alchemy, and Zosimus's study must be seen as a forerunner of a science that would create far more important and numerous miracles than the mere creation of gold from lead, a process modern scientists can now, in fact, carry out using particle accelerators or nuclear reactors—although at a cost far greater than mining and refining gold ore.

Muhammad ibn al-Khwarizmi Conceptualizes Zero

For many centuries after the appearance of mathematics, there was no concept, no symbol, for zero-ness. This lack must have greatly retarded the ability to make complex computations, or, at least, to express and further manipulate them. While an abacus can easily represent, say, the number 204 by moving two abacus beads on the wire representing hundreds, and four on the wire representing ones, how do you indicate, without the abacus, the null status of the tens?

Historians of mathematics believe that the concept of—and symbol for—zero first appeared in India about A.D. 500, specifically to indicate that the beads on one or more of the abacus wires hadn't been moved. Arab traders probably took the concept from the Hindus around 700, and, about 825, the Persian mathematician Muhammad ibn al-Khwarizmi used it in his groundbreaking algebraic text, *Hisab al-jabr w'al-musqabalah* (see "A.D. 250: Diophantus Writes the First Algebra Text"). Thus zero was conceptualized, and al-Khwarizmi gave the world a crucial tool for working with numbers at a higher level. Unfortunately, most of the world was slow to accept and appreciate this gift. Especially in backward Europe of the Dark Ages, most people continued to labor with crude arithmetical systems that had no zero.

Alhazen Establishes the Science of Optics

The scientific study of optics, which Sir Isaac Newton would elevate to its first great height in 1704, began with an Arab physicist known (much later) to Europeans as Alhazen. About 1025, he wrote that vision was the result of rays of light entering the eyes. Prior to this, the prevailing view was that the eyes emitted rays of light, which created vision.

Beyond this landmark insight (so to speak), Alhazen also experimented extensively with lenses and demonstrated that their ability to magnify images was a function of their shape, not a property of the matter of which they were composed.

1180

Alexander Neckam Introduces the Magnetic Compass to the Western World

The etymology of the word *magnet* may be traced to Magnesia, the city in Asia Minor near which (it has long been believed) a shepherd boy discovered in the sixth century B.C. that a certain ore attracted iron. While the phenomenon of magnetism was therefore long familiar, apparently no one thought to apply it to direction finding until the eleventh century A.D., even though the Chinese, as early as the second century A.D., observed that a sliver of magnetic metal, if allowed to rotate freely, always came to rest in a north-south orientation.

In 1180, an Englishman, Alexander Neckam, transmitted to Europe the ancient Chinese observation on the directional quality of magnets. Almost immediately, this led to the creation of the compass—a freely rotating magnetic needle mounted on a card inscribed with the four cardinal directions—north, south, east, and west—as well as those in between. This appropriation and new application of ancient lore empowered European navigators to explore the world and, ultimately, to dominate much of it.

An Alchemist Known Only as the False Geber Discovers Sulfuric Acid

I t is all too easy to mock medieval alchemists for confusing science with mysticism and frittering away time and effort in a hopeless search for the "philosopher's stone," a magical rock that would transform base metal into gold. But it is also true that many of the alchemists were, in fact, tireless experimenters and scholars who made valuable discoveries and who laid the foundation for modern chemistry.

We know little about most of the alchemists, and the name of one—sort of—survives only because he was associated with the discovery of the first industrially important chemical beyond those that occur naturally (such as water and air). The "False Geber" wrote a treatise around the year 1300 in which he described, among other things, sulfuric acid. It could be used to dissolve many substances, to etch metal, and to bring about a dazzling array of chemical reactions to produce many different substances.

While the False Geber, like the other alchemists, failed to transform lead into gold, he discovered a powerful acid essential to the transformation of many other things into useful substances. In this, we may see the origin of industrial chemistry.

1335

The City of Milan, Italy, Erects Perhaps the First Mechanical Clock

Time is at once the most ruthless and ephemeral dimension of the reality we know. Ancients measured it by the sun and the moon, and, about 270 B.C., the Greek inventor Ctesibius invented a water clock—the *clepsydra,* or "water stealer"—which "ran" by means of the regular dripping of water from an upper container to a lower one. This had obvious advantages over the sundial—it was usable in any weather, day or night, and it was portable—but it was still pretty clumsy and not terribly accurate.

The *clepsydra* used dripping water—that is, the force of gravity itself—to measure time, and in the fourteenth century people began to devise new ways to harness gravity—a force science had yet to name, although its effects were known intuitively—for the purpose of uniformly dividing up the day and night. Weights attached to an array of gears drove a dial on a clock face, which thereby "told" the time. Because the motive force was gravity, it was helpful to provide plenty of space for the descent of the weights. This naturally suggested a tower, which was a convenient thing, because it meant that the clock face could be fixed high up above a public square, and, in this way, the time it told could be shared by many people at once.

As clock makers became more skilled, they devised ways of linking gravity to gears, which would not only drive a clock dial, but would also audibly toll the hours, by ringing a bell. This greatly extended the range of the public clock. You didn't have to be close enough to see it, just close enough to hear it. It is believed that a tolling tower clock erected in Milan in 1335 was the first public mechanical clock.

RENAISSANCE
SCIENCE

1454

Johannes Gutenberg Invents the Modern Printing Press

Ask just about anyone to list the top two or three inventions in history, and it's almost certain that the printing press will figure among them. In itself, the "invention" of writing was a tremendous step forward (see sidebar: "The Invention of Writing, About 3500 B.C."), but writing was a laborious process and, except in the case of brief public inscriptions, the product of writing was not always easily shared among large numbers of people.

It is believed that the Chinese, by about 350, had hit upon a technology to distribute the written word more widely. They began carving characters into wooden blocks, inking them, then pressing the carved and inked blocks onto paper. The result was an impression that could be reproduced as many times as one wished. Within a few hundred years, the Chinese were printing entire books on a regular basis—while European scribes still labored to produce a few multiple copies of a work by quill and hand.

Printing came to Europe during the fourteenth century. As the Chinese had done, the first European printers carved their texts into blocks of wood—one block for each page of text. The work of carving was tedious, time-consuming, demanded great skill, and was very unforgiving of error. Once the block was carved, however, one could print as many pages as needed.

It was in 1454 that the German printer Johannes Gutenberg perfected an idea he had been working on at least since 1435. Instead of creating a uniquely carved block for each page of each book, Gutenberg decided to break the process down. Books are made of words, and words are made of letters. Gutenberg reduced the process to this basic element—the letter—and carved sets of these, which could be assembled at will into whatever words were required. Once the book was printed, the carved letters could be reused to make different words for different books. The famed Gutenberg Bible of 1454 is the first book printed using "movable type," a technology that made possible the increasingly rapid multiple production and wide distribution of an ever-growing number of books. Knowledge, which had been the exclusive property of the very few who could afford to acquire a small number of precious handwritten books, was now available to the many, and as more and more people gained access to knowledge, knowledge itself was transformed with greater and greater rapidity. Movable type moved civilization itself.

1543

Andreas Vesalius Develops the New Anatomy

Galen, a Greek physician who lived from 129 to about 199, combined his experience as a surgeon attached to a gladiatorial school with systematic dissection of animals to assemble the first attempt to account comprehensively for the human anatomy. Galen's work was extraordinary, but, of course, limited and riddled with guesswork and error. Nevertheless, in Europe, physicians relied on it through the Middle Ages. At last, in 1543, the Flemish physician Andreas Vesalius boldly dissected human cadavers and did so with unprecedented skill and thoroughness. He dared to challenge Galen, as well as all other received anatomical wisdom, and published the results of his work in *De Corporis Humani Fabrica* (On the Structure of the Human Body), which was illuminatingly illustrated by the artist Jan Stephan van Calcar, a student of no less a figure than the great painter Titian. Vesalius's *De Corporis* revolutionized medicine and the understanding of the human body.

Copernicus Proposes a Heliocentric Model of the Universe

The notion that human knowledge "progresses" from point A to point Z via an orderly course through all the letters of the alphabet is a myth. Understanding goes forward and back innumerable times. As early as 280 B.C. the Greek Aristarchus imagined that the sun was the center of the universe, and the planets, earth included, revolved around it. About 150 B.C., however, Hipparchus voiced his belief that the earth lay at the center of things and, just a few years later, Ptolemy produced the mathematics to "prove" the validity of the geocentric—the earth-centered—universe.

Human beings are by nature egocentric, and so it is not a surprise that a collective expression of egocentrism, the geocentric universe, should hold more appeal than a system centered on another heavenly body. For about sixteen centuries the Ptolemaic geocentric system was accepted as an accurate model of the way things were.

And who was in a position to disprove years of theory and tradition? After all, there was no way to get above it all, above the earth and beyond the sun, to see just what revolved around what. But there was one apparent problem with the Ptolemaic scheme. Careful observation revealed that the sun and moon moved steadily across the sky, but the planets, from time to time, seemed to reverse direction and, furthermore, grew brighter and dimmer as they traversed the sky.

Ptolemy didn't ignore the "retrograde motion" of the planets, but cobbled together exceedingly complicated mathematical explanations to account for these variations in motion. In 1507, the Polish astronomer Nicolaus Copernicus became bothered by the clumsy, inelegant mathematical contortions Ptolemy required. He couldn't prove them wrong, but he had an instinctive grasp of what modern scientists accept as a general test of a theory's validity. Provided that two different theories fully account in some way for some set of phenomena, the simpler theory is most likely to be the correct one. Copernicus just could not rest content with Ptolemy, and it occurred to him that if one returned to the view that all the planets, earth included, revolved around the sun, retrograde motion became much easier to explain as an appearance caused by the earth's own motion around the sun. Moreover, the heliocentric—sun-centered—model of the solar system also made it possible to account for why Venus and Mercury at all times remained near the sun and also why the planets appeared to grow brighter and dimmer.

Copernicus did not merely revive an ancient idea. Aristarchus had offered heliocentricism speculatively, as a way of imagining the universe. Copernicus worked it all out mathematically, and he took such care in this process that he didn't publish his work until 1543. He wanted to be very sure he was right, especially since the suggestion that the earth did not lie at the center of creation courted a charge of heresy, and, in the 1500s, the Catholic church did not hesitate to dispose of heretics—at the stake. Copernicus had the added good sense to dedicate his *De Revolutionibus Orbium Coelestium* (On the Revolution of the Heavenly Bodies) to Pope Paul III.

Despite his careful math, Copernicus hadn't gotten it completely right. He remained attached to the belief that the planets orbited in perfect circles. As Johannes Kepler would demonstrate mathematically in 1609, their orbits are ever-so-slightly elliptical. Nor did the nod to the pope prevent his book from being added to the infamous "Index"—the church's roster of books condemned as heretical. In a way, Copernicus was probably fortunate that he died immediately after *De Revolutionibus* was published in 1543. He was even more fortunate that the widespread adoption of printing (see "1454: Johannes Gutenberg Invents the Modern Printing Press") quickly circulated too many copies for the church to seize and destroy.

1545

Geronimo Cardano Conceptualizes Negative Numbers

L ike the concept of zero (see "825: Muhammad ibn al-Khwarizmi Conceptualizes Zero"), the idea of negative numbers, numbers less than zero, seems to us self-evident—yet it wasn't until 1545 that negative numbers were conceptualized in *Artis Magnae Sive de Regulis Algebraicis Liber Unus* (The Great Art), a mathematical treatise by the Italian Geronimo (or Girolamo) Cardano. Before this, people understood the concept of debt—that it was possible (all too possible) to have, in effect, less than zero funds—but, until Cardano, no one had thought of treating negative numbers as real numbers. The concept was indispensable to the development of advanced mathematics.

1545

Ambroise Paré Lays the Foundation of Modern Surgery

Beginning with the classical Greeks, science moved from the outer world to the inner world of the mind. Theory was valued over experimentation and practical knowledge. The European Middle Ages took this approach even further, and medieval scholars debated such questions as the number of teeth in a horse's mouth without deigning actually to count them.

In this cultural climate, physicians did not treat patients with surgery, which partook more of the butcher's trade than the doctor's, but left such procedures to the barber, a tradesman who doubled as a surgeon. One such was Ambroise Paré of France, who revolutionized surgical technique by lifting it, at long last, far above the level of butchery. While he did not introduce antisepsis—no one had any notion of bacteria in 1545—he did insist on cleanliness, because he found that, if the patient, the wound, and the surgeon's hands were all kept clean, the chances of postoperative infection were reduced. He had, of course, no anesthetics at his disposal, so he concentrated on formulating procedures that would be as quick, efficient, and painless as possible. Whereas most surgeons poured boiling oil into wounds as a means of cleaning them, Paré prepared soothing oils instead. While the prevailing surgical practice was to control bleeding by cauterizing severed arteries with a red-hot instrument, Paré developed the technique of tying off arteries. Not only were his procedures much less painful, they did far less damage to tissue, and the result was a significantly greater cure rate.

Fortunately for medicine, Paré described his procedures in a book. Unfortunately for sixteenth- and even seventeenth-century patients, however, Paré, a lowly barber-surgeon after all, was literate in French, but not the more learned Latin. Few physicians or scholars would descend to the vulgar tongue of the people. If Paré couldn't write it in Latin, it probably wasn't worth reading—and so the development of surgery was retarded for the next 150 years.

Rhäticus (Georg Joachim Iserin von Lauchen) Develops Trigonometry, and Erasmus Reinhold Uses It to Prepare Accurate Planetary Tables

Rhäticus—the learned pseudonym of German mathematician Georg Joachim Iserin von Lauchen—was a student of the great Copernicus, who developed the first mathematical model of a sun-centered solar system (see "1543: Copernicus Proposes a Heliocentric Model of the Universe"). To help his master calculate the orbits of the planets, Rhäticus created a set of trigonometric tables, working out the ratios of the length of the sides of triangles to each other for different angles. This provided an extraordinary tool for creating a fuller, mathematically complete model of the solar system, and, in 1551, another German mathematician, Erasmus Reinhold, used the trigonometric tables of Rhäticus to create tables by which the motions of the planets could be more precisely determined. With this, astronomy was carried beyond what one could see by looking up at the sky and began to emerge as a picture of an awesome system in dynamic motion.

Galileo, Observing Falling Bodies and Moving Bodies, Lays the Foundation of Experimental Science

Common sense is often the greatest enemy of science. A most seductive faculty, it leads us away from questioning our perceptions and lulls us into accepting as true whatever *seems* true. Thus when the great Greek philosopher Aristotle said that the heavier an object was, the faster it would fall, no one thought to question it—not only because the authority of Aristotle was rarely questioned, but also because Aristotle seemed here merely to state the obvious. The philosopher agreed with common sense.

But the Italian physicist and astronomer Galileo Galilei was not one to respect authority blindly, whether it was the authority of Aristotle or that of his own common sense.

Both, one, or neither of the following stories may be true. One story says that the Dutch mathematician Simon Stevin simultaneously dropped a heavy rock and a light one from a height. They hit the ground at exactly the same instant. The other story says that Galileo climbed the Leaning Tower of Pisa and dropped two cannonballs, one much heavier than the other, with the same result. Whichever story is true—if either is—it was Galileo and not Stevin who, in 1589, commenced a series of exacting tests to study the motion of falling objects.

It was easy enough to drop objects from a height and judge whether or not they hit the ground at the same time. However, no instruments were available in Galileo's day to measure any acceleration such objects underwent. It all happened too quickly. Therefore,

Galileo constructed an experiment that closely modeled the phenomenon he wished—but was unable—to study directly. He reasoned that the force that caused objects to fall (years later, Isaac Newton would name this force gravity) was the same that caused them to roll down an inclined plane. Both motions were downward, toward the center of the earth, but allowing the force to work at an angle rather than straight down provided sufficient time for an observer to measure, carefully and accurately, the behavior of these "falling" objects.

Galileo confirmed that (discounting wind resistance) objects fall at the same rate, regardless of weight. Aristotle and common sense were thus overturned.

He further demonstrated that objects fall at a constant, not variable, rate of acceleration, from which he reasoned that the force acting on them was constant. The conclusion Galileo drew from this was profound—and another blow to Aristotle. The Greek philosopher, again building on common sense, declared that an object would remain in motion only as long as a force was applied to it. Remove the force, and the object would come to a halt. Because all objects required a push, medieval thinkers concluded that the planets were propelled by an external force, almost certainly supplied by

The Thermometer, 1592

Just as Galileo was the first scientist to think systematically about gravity, a very basic force, so he was the first, in 1592, to create an instrument to measure the very basic sensations of hot and cold. Galileo secured a glass tube, open at one end and with a bulb blown at the other. He warmed the bulb, then placed the open end of the tube in a container of water. As the warm air within the bulb cooled, it contracted, thereby decreasing the pressure within the bulb and tube. This decrease in pressure drew the water up into the tube. If the bulb was again heated, the expanding air created an increase in pressure, which drove the column of water down. The column varied with the temperature and could be measured precisely. This thermometer was a basic scientific instrument, the purpose of which was to objectify a common and essential environmental condition.

angels. Galileo's observation of constant acceleration led him to conclude that, if friction could be discounted, an object, once set into motion, would keep moving, without the need for angelic intervention.

Galileo's observations on falling bodies added immeasurably to the science of physics and laid the foundation for the science of planetary motion. Even more important, by challenging received wisdom and common sense with a carefully constructed, infinitely repeatable experiment, Galileo created experimental science itself, the basis of all serious intellectual inquiry into the nature of the physical universe.

1590

Zacharias Janssen Invents the Microscope

B y the close of the sixteenth century, Dutch opticians were the most accomplished in the world and regularly turned out eyeglasses to correct the most common fault of human vision, nearsightedness. These convex—outwardly bowed—lenses, of course, magnified objects, and, in 1590, the Dutch lensmaker Zacharias Janssen reasoned quite simply that if one lens magnified objects x times, then the combination of two lenses would magnify them at some multiple of x times. In order to juxtapose the two lenses, he placed them at either end of a tube. In this way, he invented the microscope, which, in the next century, another Dutchman, Antonie van Leeuwenhoek, would perfect and use to study a whole new world (see "1676: Antonie van Leeuwenhoek Perfects the Microscope and Opens to Study the Universe of Microorganisms").

1608

Hans Lippershey Stumbles Upon the Telescope

Just as a Dutch optician combined two lenses to invent the microscope (see "1590: Zacharias Janssen Invents the Microscope"), another Dutch lens maker, Hans Lippershey, invented the telescope.

He didn't mean to. In 1608, he was just an apprentice spectacle maker, and, like most apprentices, spent as much time goofing off as he did working for his master. One day, he idly juxtaposed two lenses, looked through one and then through the other. He pointed them out the window, toward a distant church steeple. With a start, he saw that the steeple had been "brought" much closer to him. What's more, it had been turned upside down!

He called his master over to look. The man wisely told his apprentice to mount the lenses in a tube, and thus the telescope was born.

Word of the accidental invention spread quickly, and other lens makers assembled similar instruments. In Italy, Galileo got a hold of one right away—in 1609—pointed it at the moon, and was stunned to discover craters, mountains, and dark areas he thought were oceans (*maria*, he called them, using the Latin word for seas). Directed at just this single heavenly body, the telescope shattered a much-cherished vision of the moon as a glowing orb of light, a perfect fixture in God's heaven. Galileo saw that it was a world, scarred and imperfect, not unlike the earth itself.

1614

John Napier Develops the Concept of the Logarithm

Arithmetic is necessary to the work of the mathematician and scientist, but the work of calculation is often tedious and time-consuming. By streamlining arithmetical mechanics, mathematicians may broaden the scope of their creative vision. Early in the seventeenth century, the Scottish mathematician John Napier realized that the great labor-saving expedient known as the exponent could be expanded to save even more work. In exponential form, 3×3 is written 3^2. In multiplying exponential numbers, we may just add the exponents instead of multiplying the numbers. Thus $2^2 \times 2^4$ may be expressed as 2×2 (4) added to $2 \times 2 \times 2 \times 2$ (16) equals 64. Or it may be expressed $2^2 \times 2^4 = 2^6$. The sum of the exponents is 6. In this way, multiplication can be simplified to addition and, likewise, division can be simplified to subtraction.

Working with exponents in this way is easy, provided that the exponents are whole numbers. For example, 2^4 is 16, and 2^5 is 32. But how do we derive, exponentially, the numbers in between 16 and 32? If there were an easy way to obtain the exponents between the whole numbers, all multiplication could be handled as addition, and all division as subtraction. This would greatly reduce and simplify the arithmetic and let mathematicians devote themselves to math.

Napier created formulas that enabled him to get at the numbers between the whole numbers. With these, he developed tables of what he called *logarithms* (Greek for "proportionate numbers"), which mathematicians and scientists could use to simplify and therefore speed their work, enabling them to get more done, more accurately, with greater speed, and in realms of increasing complexity. In the years, decades, and centuries before computers, Napier's logarithms energized all branches of inquiry requiring complex and extensive calculation.

1620

Francis Bacon Proposes the Scientific Method

In 1620, the daring British philosopher Francis Bacon published *Novum Organum,* or *The New Organon,* an answer to the much venerated *Organon* of Aristotle, the book that had dictated the rules of philosophy—and, therefore, the rules of science as well—since it was written, about 350 B.C. Where Aristotle had extolled the sovereign authority of deductive reasoning for all inquiry, Bacon declared that while deduction worked for mathematics, it was inadequate for scientific inquiry. This, he proposed, required induction—generalization based on a mass of precise observation derived from actual experience and deliberate experiment. In short, Bacon proposed what has come to be called the scientific method: knowledge arrived at through experiment analyzed inductively. It was a bold proposal, which has had a profound and well-nigh universal impact not only on science, but on thought itself.

Willebrord Snel Creates the Science of Refraction

People have been using and manipulating lenses of various sorts since at least the days of classical Greece, but it wasn't until the early seventeenth century that anyone thought of studying the action of lenses systematically—which is to say, mathematically. In 1621, the Dutch mathematician Willebrord Snel founded the science of refraction, which is the foundation of practical optics, by demonstrating that the sine of the angle to the vertical of light leaving a lens is in a constant relationship with the sine of the angle to the vertical of the light that hits the surface of the lens. Armed with this mathematical constant, lens makers could now design a wide array of lenses and lens assemblies for many purposes.

1624

Jan Baptista van Helmont Coins the Term *Gas* to Describe Matter in "Chaos"

As the classical Greeks saw it, physical reality was made up of four earthly elements—earth, water, fire, and air—and one heavenly element, aether (the word means, roughly, "blazing"). This view remained largely unquestioned for many centuries, well into the seventeenth century. In the 1620s, however, the Flemish physician Jan Baptista van Helmont worked experimentally with a number of vapors. His observations made it apparent to him that not all vapors behaved in the same way as air did and, in fact, one vapor behaved differently from another. By 1624, Helmont decided that the various vapors formed a unique class of substance. For all their differences, they shared certain salient characteristics, the most striking of which was that they had no specific volume, but did fill any container. Thus Helmont concluded that vapors were matter in utter *chaos*. Transliterating that Greek word in tune with his Flemish ear, Helmont created the term *gas*.

In time, the concept of gas drew scientists away from the classical Greek picture of the five elements. Instead, they depicted matter in states—solid, liquid, and gaseous—and this made room for the modern vision of many elements, all of which may exist, depending on external conditions, in solid, liquid, or gaseous state.

William Harvey Describes the Circulation of Blood

In the centuries after Galen, a number of physicians attempted to describe the circulation of blood, but they could not fully account for the fact that the heart is a double pump. A popular early view was that one portion of the heart fed the lungs, while the other part supplied blood to the rest of the body. The details, of course, were never worked out—mainly because this view, though pervasive, was just plain wrong.

As a student of the Italian physician Girolamo Fabrici, Harvey had learned of valves in the veins that kept blood flowing in one direction only. Armed with this knowledge, Harvey experimented with animals. He tied off a vein and noted that blood accumulated in the vein on the side away from the heart even as it simultaneously piled up in an artery on the side toward the heart. From this, Harvey concluded that blood flowed away from the heart in the arteries and toward the heart via the veins. He continued his experiments and observations until he had accumulated enough data to publish in 1628 a slim, concise volume titled *Exercitatio Anatomica de Motu Cordis et Sanguinis in Animalibus* (On the Movement of the Heart and the Blood in Animals). In it, he traced the circulation of blood from the right ventricle of the heart to the lungs, and, ultimately, back to the left ventricle. From here, it is pumped out to the body generally, whence it returns to the right ventricle—all in continual circulation.

The stodgy medical establishment of the seventeenth century

was slow to accept Harvey's elegant picture of circulation, but the physician did have the satisfaction of seeing it generally accepted before he died in 1657. That was certainly gratifying. But even Harvey didn't grasp the magnitude of what he had done, which was to create the modern science of physiology.

Galileo Is Charged with Heresy

alileo was a great scientist and a man of principle. However, he was also a practical realist. His reason and his own observations had led him to accept the view of Copernicus, that the earth and the other planets orbited the sun in a heliocentric—sun-centered—solar system (see "1543: Copernicus Proposes a Heliocentric Model of the Universe"). However, Galileo also understood that to espouse this point of view in Italy, which was dominated by the Catholic church, was dangerous indeed. The position of the church was unalterably geocentric—earth-centered—and to assert anything contrary to this was to be guilty of heresy, a crime punishable by burning at the stake.

At last, in 1632, Urban VIII ascended the papal throne. Because Urban was a friend of Galileo's, the scientist felt emboldened to publish a book he hoped would promote and explain definitively and once and for all the logical superiority of the Copernican view versus the geocentric view. Galileo's *Dialogue on the Two Chief World Systems,* published in 1632, was not a sober-sided scientific treatise, but a spirited and witty dialogue among an advocate of the Ptolemaic, earth-centered system, a champion of Copernicus's heliocentric view, and a seeker of enlightenment.

Of course, the Copernican view won out—and that might not have been so bad, except that Galileo's book was so entertaining that it reached not just scientists and the learned minority, but that portion of the masses who were at least literate. Despite their friendship, Urban became alarmed, and, in 1633, hauled Galileo before the Inquisition to answer for his heresy. Perhaps because Urban was indeed his friend, Galileo was not punished. At age seventy,

Galileo Galilei was not interested in a trip to the rack, much less the stake. On June 22, 1633, he renounced the heliocentric picture, "admitting" to the Inquisitors that not the sun, but the earth, was at the center of the universe. Thus Galileo was released to a loose form of house arrest. Nevertheless, it is said that, as Galileo turned away from the Inquisitors, he muttered under his breath, "and yet it moves."

In a way, June 22, 1633, was a victory for coercive superstition and a dark day for the freedom of scientific inquiry. Yet it was a pyrrhic victory. Those who thought seriously about such things understood that Galileo had actually renounced nothing, and, thanks to the printing press, there were too many copies of his *Dialogue* in circulation to collect and destroy. Not only was the heliocentric model of the solar system taking ever firmer hold on the learned world, the spirit of scientific inquiry was stealing the march on received wisdom and superstition masquerading in the guise of religion.

ENLIGHTENMENT
SCIENCE

1642

Blaise Pascal Invents a Practical Adding Machine

The abacus (see sidebar: "The Abacus, About 500 B.C.") was almost certainly the earliest computer—if we take the term *computer* to include machines that do nothing more than calculate. The first significant advance in mechanical computing beyond the abacus did not come until more than 2,100 years after the Egyptians began using the device. In 1642, the French mathematician Blaise Pascal crafted a genuine calculating machine. It was an arrangement of wheels, each marked off from one to ten. When the right-most wheel, which represented ones, made a complete revolution, it engaged the wheel immediately to its left, which represented tens, and advanced it a single notch. That wheel engaged another, to its left, moving it a single notch when ten tens had been reached. This third wheel represented hundreds. And thus the wheels progressed through hundreds, thousands, and so on.

Pascal hoped to grow rich from his calculating machine, which he tinkered with from 1642 until 1649, when he produced a version he deemed worthy of a patent. The machine offered speedy calculations without the possibility of error—provided, of course, the information entered was correct. But the world was not yet eager for a calculating machine, and Pascal's pioneering computer never saw commercial success.

1661

Robert Boyle Lays the Foundation of Modern Chemistry

Jan Baptista van Helmont's description of gases (see "1624: Jan Baptista van Helmont Coins the Term *Gas* to Describe Matter in 'Chaos'") had begun to undermine the long-cherished belief that the earth consisted of four elements, fire, water, earth, and air, and the heavens of a fifth, aether, but this view nevertheless persisted well into the seventeenth century, greatly retarding the progress of chemistry, which continued to be dominated by alchemists—who were more sorcerer than scientist. The feisty Irish chemist and physicist Robert Boyle aggressively attacked both the dominance of the five-element view and the hegemony of the alchemist with his 1661 book *The Skeptical Chymist.* In it, he made three seminal points: First, he established chemistry as a field in its own right, distinct from the area of inquiry that had hitherto dominated it, medicine. Second, he held that chemistry could not be built on received wisdom, tradition, or even deduction. It had to be, he argued, an experimental science. Third, he proposed as the first appropriate goal of experimentation the discovery of the true elements. The fire, water, air, earth, aether model, he pointed out, did not adequately account for reality. An element, Boyle stated, was a substance that could not be simplified or broken down. Therefore, anything that could not be reduced to constituents was an element, and any candidate for elementary status had to be shown to be incapable of reduction to simpler constituents. Thus Boyle not only gave the concept of elements its modern definition, he provided a goal and purpose for the new science of chemistry—no longer to search for a way to convert lead into gold, but to discover just what substances made up the foundation of the physical world. And the only way to do this was by tireless experimentation.

1666

Isaac Newton Describes the Visible Spectrum

Twenty-four-year-old Isaac Newton turned his prodigious intellect to the subject of light and discovered that white light, assumed to be the embodiment of purity itself, was actually composed of a spectrum of colors. The discovery was made when Newton methodically experimented with prisms. He observed that white light passing through a prism was broken into red, orange, yellow, green, blue, and violet, always in that order, beginning with the portion of the light that is least bent by the prism, red.

Newton was surely not the first person to pass light through a prism, but he was the first to draw conclusions from it. First, while others had assumed that the breakup of light into colors was due to some property of glass, Newton turned the focus back on the light itself, where it belonged. When he allowed the light to pass through two prisms, it entered the first, broke up into the color spectrum, then entered the second and emerged as white light again. Color, therefore, was a property of light, not glass. From this, Newton made one of the great quantum leaps of scientific reasoning, concluding that the phenomenon of color results from the property of various matter to absorb some portions of the spectrum and to reflect others. In short, *all* color was ultimately a property of light. The perception of color was the result of the action of light on matter.

1668

John Wallis Formulates the Law of Conservation of Momentum, First of the Laws of Conservation That Are Fundamental to Our Understanding of the Universe

Our world is never static. It is, rather, dynamic, its varied constituents always in motion. We grow up with an intuitive understanding of movement (the Latin word for movement is *momentum*), learning by experience that kicking a soccer ball will send it far, but kicking a nice, round boulder will result in very sore toes. A big part of science is the rationalization and quantification of intuition, and momentum, long understood intuitively, was not explored mathematically until the Englishman John Wallis formulated his law of conservation of momentum in 1668.

It goes like this: Momentum is the product of mass multiplied by velocity. Momentum is neither created nor destroyed. It is merely transferred. Thus, in a closed system, a system in which no momentum is introduced from the outside nor any momentum is allowed to "leak" to the outside, the total momentum remains constant.

Understanding momentum intellectually—not just intuitively—enables many useful calculations concerning motion, which in turn makes it possible to design a vast array of machines, to calculate the energy required to accomplish various tasks, and to predict what will happen if the momentum of a Volkswagen Beetle meets that of an eighteen-wheel Peterbilt. Even more profoundly, understanding the law of conservation of momentum, that momentum is neither created nor destroyed, but merely transferred, contributes immeasurably to an understanding of the universe itself.

1668

Francesco Redi Disproves Spontaneous Generation

Most of us are disgusted by the sight of decomposition—the carcass by the side of the road, crawling with thousands of maggots. Yet, for centuries, people thought there was something miraculous about such a scene. Whereas the creation of human life and the more complex forms of animal life clearly required the mating of male and female, a long gestation period, and a dramatic episode of birth, some forms of life apparently sprang forth spontaneously from decaying matter. Let meat decay, and maggots appeared; their generation, as far as anybody could tell, was spontaneous.

Scientists look on the universe with a combination of wonder and skepticism. They are willing to be amazed, but, first, they need to test what everyone else simply assumes. Thus, in 1668, the Italian physician Francesco Redi designed an experiment to test spontaneous generation.

He took eight glass flasks and put into each a variety of meats. Four of the flasks he sealed. Four he left exposed. Only the exposed meat, on which flies could land, revealed the presence of maggots. Like the exposed meat, the sealed meat turned putrid—but it "produced" no maggots.

It occurred to Redi that the absence of sufficient air in the sealed flasks might have interfered with the process of spontaneous generation, so he redesigned the experiment, repeating it, but without sealing any of the flasks. Instead, he covered four with gauze, sufficient to exclude flies, but clearly porous enough to let in plenty of air. Once again, only the meat in the fully exposed flasks became infested. Thus Redi had created the first documented biological experiment employing "controls"—measures to ensure that the effect under study is produced by the cause under study, and not by something incidentally or accidentally introduced by the experimenter.

Even more important, Redi had provided experimental evidence for one of the bedrock principles of modern biology: All life comes from life and only from life.

1669

Newton and Gottfried Wilhelm Leibniz Independently Invent Calculus

I t may be the most famous moment in science. In 1665, young Isaac Newton had taken refuge on his mother's farm from the deadly bubonic plague that held London in its grip. Legend has it that Newton was reading under a tree when an apple fell on his head. According to Newton himself, however, he was gazing out of a window at a brilliantly moonlit night. The moon was so bright that he clearly saw an apple fall from a tree. It occurred to him in that moment: Why does an apple fall to earth, while the moon does not?

He reasoned that the moon was not exempt from gravity, and that, in fact, it *did* fall. However, because the moon was also moving horizontally, it fell exactly enough, from moment to moment, to make up for the curvature of the earth. Moving forward, the moon fell perpetually, thereby orbiting the earth—neither falling into it, nor shooting out, on a tangent, away from it.

Newton understood that this theory, brilliant though it was, meant little until it could be described mathematically. But the mathematical tools available to Newton were insufficient to produce the calculations he needed. How could he calculate a problem in which *all* of the earth, at every point, exerted a gravitational force on every point of the moon? Since both the earth and the moon have considerable volume—and are not the hypothetical spaceless points of mathematics—the force of gravity is exerted from a range of different distances and angles. Nothing existed to work such a complex problem.

So Newton set about inventing the tools he needed. In 1669, he began developing calculus, a method of dealing with multiple relationships, with limits and the differentiation and integration of functions of one or more variables. Calculus is ideal for working with bodies in motion, whose relationship to one another is dynamic.

Unknown to Newton, in Germany, the mathematician Gottfried Wilhelm Leibniz was also developing calculus. Newton probably beat him to the punch, but Leibniz created a more flexible and useful symbolic language by which problems could be expressed and resolved. At the time—and for some years afterward—proud Brits sparred with proud Germans in a struggle over who should be given credit for opening the door to higher mathematics. By now, that controversy has long been laid to rest, and both Newton and Leibniz are credited with having developed, independently from each other, calculus.

1675

Olaus Rømer Calculates the Approximate Speed of Light

A t least as early as Galileo, there was curiosity about the speed of light. The Italian tried to measure it by stationing himself, with a lantern, atop one hill and a friend, also equipped with a lantern, on another. Once he and his friend were in place, Galileo would slide open his lantern, exposing his flame. His counterpart on the distant hill was to expose his flame as soon as he saw Galileo's. Galileo would time the delay between the exposure and the response and, from this, calculate the speed of light. The trouble was that, no matter how far apart the two men stationed themselves, the result was always the same. Galileo drew two conclusions: First, any elapsed time he measured represented nothing more than the time it took his counterpart to react to the sight of his light. The measurement had to do with physiology, not physics. Second, light traveled too fast to measure practically; indeed, some argued that light moved with infinite speed.

Almost a hundred years after Galileo threw in the towel concerning the speed of light, the Danish astronomer Olaus Rømer revisited the problem. He had not intended to do so, but something he observed awakened his curiosity. He was working at the Paris Observatory, studying the motions of Jupiter's moons. The Italian astronomer Gian Domenico Cassini had, about ten years earlier, timed these motions carefully, especially noting just when each moon passed behind Jupiter and was therefore eclipsed. Scientists learn much from repeating the experiments and observations of others. Like Cassini, Rømer timed the eclipses. To his profound surprise, his figures differed from Cassini's. And there was even more: The eclipses came progressively earlier during the season at which the earth was closer to Jupiter than when its orbit was receding from Jupiter's.

In science, discovery sometimes comes in great leaps and momentous revelations, but even more often it comes from recognizing subtle differences in minute measurements. Rømer theorized that the variation in timing came about because the light he saw had to travel farther when the Earth and Jupiter were farther apart; therefore, light must have a finite, and not an infinite, speed. Using what he knew about the distance separating the earth from Jupiter, Rømer calculated the speed of light at 141,000 miles per second.

He was, in fact, wrong. The speed of light is approximately 186,000 miles per second. Yet he was not *very* wrong, getting within almost 76 percent of the correct answer—and doing so based on the observation of a single phenomenon.

1676

Antonie vanLeeuwenhoek Perfects the Microscope and Opens to Study the Universe of Microorganisms

The Dutch lens maker Antonie van Leeuwenhoek did not invent the microscope (see "1590: Zacharias Janssen Invents the Microscope"), and he was not even the first to use it to investigate the structure of life, but he did build a microscope of unprecedented power—creating exquisitely ground lenses capable of 200 times magnification—and he used it to open many views of a hitherto unknown world.

In 1676, Leeuwenhoek put under his lens a drop of pond water. What he expected to see we don't know. But what he actually saw amazed him: The droplet was alive with myriad microoranisms—Leeuwenhoek called them animalicules—entirely invisible to the naked eye.

The "Cell" Described, 1665

In 1665, the English scientist Robert Hooke used the microscope to examine a dazzling array of specimens and produced a beautifully illustrated compendium of his observations in the 1665 book *Micrographia*. His single most fascinating observation was the result of examining a paper-thin slice of cork. Hooke noted that the cork consisted of tiny rectangular holes, which, because they reminded Hooke of little rooms, he called *cells*. To be strictly accurate, Hooke had not discovered the cells themselves, but their remains—their dead shell, as it were. In a living specimen—not dead cork—each rigid cell would be filled with fluid (cytoplasm) around a nucleus and other structures (organelles). Nevertheless, Hooke had coined the term, alerting other scientists to this all-important structural and physiological constituent of plant and animal life.

1687

Newton Publishes the *Principia,* in Which He Formulates Three Laws of Motion

In 1669, Isaac Newton developed calculus as a tool for explaining how the moon orbited the earth by, in effect, perpetually falling toward it (see "1669: Newton and Gottfried Wilhelm Leibniz Independently Invent Calculus"). This led in 1687 to the publication of *Philosophiae Naturalis Principia Mathematica* (Mathematical Principles of Natural Philosophy), usually called simply the *Principia.* In this volume, perhaps the single greatest book ever written on a scientific subject, Newton explained not just how the moon orbited the earth, but why the planets maintained their orbits and why these orbits were elliptical. To arrive at this explanation, he had to codify, mathematically, Galileo's observations on falling bodies (see "1589: Galileo, Observing Falling Bodies and Moving Bodies, Lays the Foundation of Experimental Science"), proposing three Laws of Motion.

The first law sets forth the principle of inertia: A body at rest remains at rest and a body in motion remains in motion at a constant velocity until an outside force or forces act upon it.

The second law defines force as the product of mass times acceleration.

The third law holds that for every action there is an equal and opposite reaction.

From these three laws, Newton derived the basic mathematics of modern physics, and others who followed him used them as the basis for describing virtually all mechanical effects, from simple machines to the motions of celestial bodies.

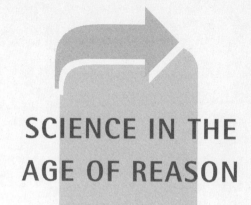

SCIENCE IN THE
AGE OF REASON

1712

Thomas Newcomen Invents
a Practical Steam Engine

The motive power of steam was first demonstrated about A.D. 50 by the Greek engineer Hero. His "steam engine" was a hollow sphere from which two bent tubes protruded, their openings pointing in opposing directions. The sphere was filled with water and heated. When the water boiled, the escaping steam propelled the sphere, causing it to rotate.

Hero's engine was a brilliant little device, but no one thought of putting it to any practical use, and it wasn't until some seventeen centuries later that the British engineer Thomas Newcomen invented a practical, if quite inefficient, steam engine, in which the steam was used to push a piston and, in its initial application, drive a pump to eject water from coal mines.

Lady Mary Wortley Montagu Introduces Inoculation into Europe

Smallpox, one of the great epidemic scourges of humankind, was doubly cruel. Many died from it; however, most people survived the attack, only to emerge from it badly disfigured by pockmarks, deep scars left by myriad pustules. The only mercy the disease showed was this: If one survived, one never contracted smallpox again. And then there were also certain fortunate people who contracted only a mild form of the disease. This left them only slightly disfigured, if at all, and yet conferred exactly the same immunity as in major cases.

People would sometimes seek out an individual suffering from mild smallpox, get close to him, and hope to contract the disease—in its mild form. In Turkey, by the eighteenth century, some people were going a step further. They pricked a pustule from an individual who had contracted a mild case of smallpox, then scratched the matter into the skin of a healthy person, thereby *inoculating* him or her with the disease. Lady Mary Wortley Montagu, a poet and the wife of Britain's ambassador to Turkey, noted that, most of the time, those inoculated suffered only a mild case. *Most* of the time. She also noted that, occasionally, the person inoculated would come down with a severe case, either fatal or disfiguring. Nevertheless, she was sufficiently impressed with inoculation to bring news of it back to England, where many people were willing to risk death or disfigurement by deliberate infection rather than wait for the disease to do its evil work in its own time.

Edmond Halley Describes the Movement of Stars

Nothing in creation seems more permanent than the stars. Although the planets, the sun, and the moon move (or seem to move) relative to the stars, the stars themselves remain fixed. This had been believed since ancient times, and thus the heavens were called the "firmament."

It is the business of scientists to question accepted perceptions of reality, and it is, in particular, the business of astronomers to make seemingly impossible observations. To practically everyone the stars always appeared motionless. To look at the night sky, night after night, was, apparently, to confirm this universally held notion. However, the great British astronomer Edmond Halley took a different view. He carefully determined the position of the very bright stars Sirius, Procyon, and Arcturus. He compared what he observed with the positions recorded by the ancient Greeks thousands of years earlier. There was a marked difference. Even more tellingly, there was a difference between his observations in 1718 and those made by the famously careful astronomer Tycho Brahe in the late sixteenth century.

From his observations and those of the past, Halley concluded that the stars moved, and that only their great distance from earth made them appear to stand still. This conclusion, built on careful observation and close comparison with the observations of others over time, was a revolution in how we perceive the universe and our place in it. The cosmic stability promised by the ancients, by the church, and even by the testimony of our own senses was a fiction. A new vision emerged.

Stephen Gray Experiments with Electrical Conduction

Early eighteenth-century "natural philosophers" (as scientists generally called themselves) were fascinated by static electricity and performed an array of experiments to explore it. One of the most important was that of the British scientist Stephen Gray, who, in 1729, found that if he generated a static charge in a long glass tube, corks stoppering either end of the tube were also charged, even though they had not been directly contacted. Gray concluded from this that electricity traveled, and, to find out just how far, he used long lengths of twine to conduct charges. He induced a charge to travel as much as 800 feet.

Gray believed that electricity was a type of fluid substance and that its fluid nature enabled it to travel. Moreover, the fluid theory explained (as far as Gray was concerned) why electricity traveled more easily in some substances than it did in others. Later experimenters built on this observation, deeming some substances "conductors" and others "nonconductors."

1735

Carolus Linnaeus Creates a Taxonomy

The Swedish naturalist Carl von Linné—who always signed his scientific work with the Latinized form of his name, Carolus Linnaeus—was not the first person to attempt the systematic classification of plant and animal life, but he did so in a way that was more thorough and useful than what any of his predecessors had produced.

In 1735, Linnaeus's *Systema Naturae* presented a classification of a dazzling catalogue of plants. His system grouped living things into a nesting set of classifications, beginning with the broadest, *kingdom*. Linnaeus distinguished only two of these, plant and animal. Next came *phylum*, then *class, order, family, genus,* and *species*. Plants or animals (in later editions of *Systema Naturae*, Linnaeus classified animals as well as plants) of related classes were put into the same phylum; those of related orders were put into the same class; of related families into the same order; and so on, down the line narrowing toward greater and greater specificity.

Taxonomy Before Linneaus, 1686 and 1691

In 1686, John Ray, a British naturalist, published his classification of some 18,600 plant species in a way that pointed toward ideas of evolution by underscoring the relationships among various species. Ray did the same for animal species in 1691, isolating the most telling characteristics that relate one type of animal to another. Although Ray's classification was neither as thorough nor as systematically cohesive as that of Linnaeus, it was the first attempt at a truly scientific classification.

From the last two categories, genus and species, came the Latin name of the plant or animal. So compelling was this system that biologists still use it, and, therefore, human beings are still known as *Homo sapiens*. The genus is *Homo,* the species *sapiens*. This is known as binomial nomenclature.

What's in a name?

By looking at plant and animal life as he did, Linnaeus introduced an orderly way of looking at life, a way that both invited and demanded drawing connections between organisms that were clearly related, yet also differentiated. This approach paved the way for an evolutionary view of life on earth, because it suggested that individual species branch out from common genera, which, in turn, evolve from even more common families, and so on, *up* the line of classifications. The implication is that some common ancestor or precursor once existed from which all the variety of life developed over many, many years.

1745

Pieter van Musschenbroek Invents the Leyden Jar, a Device for Storing Electricity

The varied phenomena of static electricity had fascinated people since at least the time of the ancient Greeks, and, early in the eighteenth century, Francis Hauksbee, a British physicist, invented a simple machine (a glass sphere turned by a crank) to generate static electric charges at will. But the first significant advance in the manipulation of electricity was made by the Dutch physicist Pieter van Musschenbroek at the University of Leyden.

The device, which came to be called a Leyden jar, was a metal container hung from insulating silk cords and containing water. A brass wire pierced a cork that stoppered the container and terminated in the water. Static electricity could be generated outside the Leyden jar, and the charge conducted through the brass wire and into the water. The Leyden jar *stored* the charge—which could be released (discharged) as a great spark if any grounded object was brought near the brass wire. If that object happened to be a human finger, the discharge produced a painful jolt of electricity.

The Leyden jar was a curiosity that swept Europe, but it was also a tool that interested serious experimenters, including Benjamin Franklin (see "1752: Benjamin Franklin Tames Lightning").

Jean-Antoine Nollet Describes Osmosis, Thereby Laying the Foundation for a Theory of Molecular Behavior

The word *osmosis* is derived from a Greek root, meaning "to push." It is an apt description of a phenomenon first noted by the French natural philosopher Jean-Antoine Nollet in 1748. He filled a small container with an alcohol solution, covered it with a portion of pig bladder, then immersed this in a tub of water. He observed that, over time, the bladder bulged and, eventually, burst.

Nollet correctly concluded from his observations that more water entered the alcohol solution than left it, thereby building up pressure against the bladder. He further concluded that this meant that the water alone could penetrate the bladder membrane, but that once it was in solution with the alcohol, it could not penetrate the bladder—so it pushed against it, causing it to distend and, finally, to burst.

Why this should be the case, Nollet could not explain. He did not understand that what he was really observing was the behavior of molecules of different sizes. The relatively small molecules of pure water could pass through the bladder membrane, whereas the relatively large water-alcohol molecules could not. Nevertheless, the observation of osmosis laid the groundwork for a theory of molecular behavior, which would begin to emerge by the end of the eighteenth century.

1749

Georges-Louis Leclerc de Buffon Estimates the Age of the Earth

The most respected naturalist of his age, Buffon was given to sweeping speculations that, while grossly inaccurate in their specifics, foreshadowed the profound discoveries of a later age. It was Buffon who was the first to propose a theory of evolution, although his theory might be more properly called a theory of devolution. For he believed that species became differentiated from one another not through a process of positive development, but through one analogous to rotting or decay, degeneration. Thus, to Buffon, donkeys were descended from horses; that is, they were a species of degenerate horse. Similarly, apes were a degenerated species of human beings.

In the same massive work in which he discussed evolution/devolution, his multivolume *Natural History,* Buffon also speculated on the age of the earth. His theory was that the earth and the other planets had been formed by the collision of the sun with a comet— which he thought of as an extremely massive object. If this indeed had been the case, Buffon reasoned, it should be possible to determine the age of the earth by calculating how long it would take an object the size of the earth to cool from a temperature approaching that of the sun to the planet's present temperature. By his calculations, the earth was 75,000 years old. And he took this figure a step further by calculating not just how long it would take the earth to cool to its present temperature, but how long it would take for it to cool sufficiently to support life. He pegged this at about 35,000 years. Furthermore, taking his calculations forward, Buffon estimated that the earth, continuing to cool, would reach a frigid temperature incompatible with life in about 90,000 years.

All of Buffon's figures, we now know, were wildly wrong. Yet he had taken an important step away from theology and into science. In Genesis, all creation spans just six days. Buffon's observations and reasoning concerning evolution and the age of the earth suggested that the sun and at least one other object (the "comet") existed before the earth. The earth required thousands of years to cool sufficiently to support life. Life itself appeared, then evolved (or degenerated).

Not only did Buffon's picture of creation span far longer than the biblical six days, it all must have predated the biblical creation. In 1650, the Anglican bishop James Ussher used the ages of the prophets and other hints in the Old Testament to calculate the date of creation. It came out to 4004 B.C. In 1654, another British theologian, John Lightfoot, pinpointed creation to October 26, 4004 B.C., at 9 A.M. Buffon's evidence indicated a date much, much earlier.

René-Antoine Ferchault de Réaumur Describes the Process of Digestion in Animals

Some science is driven by pure curiosity—How does *this* work? What does *that* mean?—whereas some science is driven by the nagging need to settle an argument.

For many years, naturalists had debated the process of digestion. By the eighteenth century, there were essentially two opposed points of view. One held that digestion was mainly a mechanical process, in which the stomach, through muscular action, ground up food. The other view argued that digestion was mainly chemical in nature, perhaps a variety of fermentation.

René-Antoine Ferchault de Réaumur was a physicist, not a biologist or physiologist, but he hit upon an ingenious experiment to settle the debate. He knew that hawks tore at their prey, swallowing down large chunks of meat, digesting some of it, and regurgitating what could not be digested. As Réaumur saw it, this habit of regurgitation made the hawk an ideal experimental subject. He put meat in a small metal cylinder. The ends of the cylinder were covered with gauze. Réaumur forced the hawk to swallow the cylinder and, after a time, the bird regurgitated it. Examining the meat, Réaumur observed that it had been extensively dissolved. Because the meat had been encapsulated in the cylinder, Réaumur knew that this dissolution could not have been the result of any mechanical grinding. Therefore, it must be the product of a chemical process. But what kind of chemical?

Réaumur devised a second experiment to find out. He induced

the hawk to swallow an indigestible sponge, which it duly regurgitated after a time, soaked through with digestive juices. Réaumur squeezed out the contents of the sponge, placed a piece of meat in the fluid and watched as the fluid began to dissolve the food. Réaumur concluded that the stomach secretes an acid, which digests food. To demonstrate that this was not peculiar to hawks, he repeated the experiment with dogs.

1752

Benjamin Franklin Tames Lightning

L ike another of the Founding Fathers, Thomas Jefferson, Benjamin Franklin was as interested in science as he was in government and diplomacy. Also like Jefferson, Franklin was a man of brilliance and brilliant insight.

Attracted to the phenomena of electricity, Franklin experimented with static charges and Leyden jars (see "1745: Pieter van Musschenbroek Invents the Leyden Jar, a Device for Storing Electricity"). It was Franklin who first proposed the concepts of negative and positive charges, suggesting that negative charges repelled each other, as did positive charges, but a positive charge was drawn to a negative. True, Franklin thought (as did others) that electricity was a fluid. What he called *positive electricity* was an excess of electric fluid. What he called *negative electricity* was a deficiency of fluid. Obviously, an excess of fluid is repelled by another excess of fluid. Likewise, a deficiency of fluid cannot be attracted to another deficiency, because neither could bring anything to the other. But an excess of fluid would naturally flow toward a deficiency.

Like everyone else at the time, Franklin was wrong about the fluid nature of electricity, but he had provided, in the idea of positive and negative charges, a valuable insight into how electricity behaves.

More dramatic was the intuitive association he made between static electricity and lightning. When a static charge that had been transferred to a Leyden jar was "drawn off" by bringing a conducting object close to the wire protruding from the jar, a spark and crackle were produced. Franklin reasoned that these were, in essence, miniature lightning and thunder discharges. To test his hypothesis, in 1751, he launched a kite into a thunderstorm. He had fitted a metal rod to the kite, because he knew metal was a conductor, and he ran down from the rod a long silk thread. Attached to that thread, which was soon soaked in the rain, was another dry silk thread, tied to a brass key. As the storm raged, Franklin observed that the fibers of the dry silk threat began to stand up, repelling each other, thereby indicating that a charge was traveling through the thread. Franklin brought his knuckle near the key, and a spark arced from the key to his knuckle. When he brought the key into contact with the wire from a Leyden jar, the jar became charged. Thus Franklin demonstrated that lightning is an electrical discharge.

If Franklin was a brilliant theoretician, he was even sharper when it came to the practical application of theory. His kite experiment had shown him that the electrical charge of lighting could be conducted artificially. Lightning was responsible for many fires in colonial America. Anything tall—especially church steeples—were often set ablaze by lightning strikes. In 1752, in the pages of his famed *Poor Richard's Almanack,* Franklin proposed that a long metal rod be fastened to the tallest part of a building, and a wire run down from the rod, away from the building, and into the ground. The lighting, always attracted to the tallest conductor, would strike the rod rather than the building, and its charge would be conducted, harmlessly, down the wire and dissipated in the ground. The lightning rod had been born, and a destructive natural force tamed—at least to a significant degree.

1766

Albrecht von Haller Establishes the Science of Neurology

Greek anatomists recognized the existence of nerves, but believed they served as a kind of circulatory system, conveying a fluid the nature and function of which were unknown to Western medicine. This nonexplanation had been accepted for centuries before the Swiss physiologist Albrecht von Haller began to experiment with nerves.

Actually, he began with muscle tissue freshly dissected from an animal. He demonstrated that muscle was *irritable*. That is, a slight stimulus to the exposed muscle would cause it to contract. But Haller took this further, demonstrating that if a nerve connected to the muscle was stimulated, the muscle would contract even more dramatically. Furthermore, the muscle would contract even if a very, very small stimulus was applied to the nerve—smaller than that required to induce contraction when it was applied directly to the muscle. From this, von Haller concluded that, in a living animal, stimulation of the nerves—not of the muscles—caused and controlled muscular movement.

Haller went another step further. Noting that all the nerves ultimately went to the brain or the spinal cord, both of which had been identified long ago as the centers of sensation and perception, Haller concluded that nerves were not only responsible for causing and regulating movement, but for generating sensation, which was processed by the brain. In almost a single stroke, therefore, Haller founded neurology, the science of nerves, the nervous system, and the brain.

1772

Antoine-Laurent Lavoisier
Describes Combustion

Up through most of the eighteenth century, chemists cared remarkably little about making precise measurements. They combined substances and noted the results. The French chemist Antoine-Laurent Lavoisier took what was a new approach by measuring quantities with great precision before and after a chemical process. In 1772, he applied this technique—call it quantitative chemistry—to the problem of combustion. The leading theory of combustion held that combustible objects were rich in a substance called *phlogiston* (from the Greek, "to set on fire"). Burning consumed phlogiston, leaving as a residue that portion of a substance deficient in phlogiston.

As proof of the phlogiston theory, the German chemist George Ernst Stahl pointed out that combustible materials lose mass (as evidenced by the fact that they weigh less) when burned. The lost mass was assumed to be due to the consumption of phlogiston. Stahl did not address an important contradiction in this theory, however. To his credit, he believed that the rusting of metal was a form of the same process that takes place during combustion. (Today, it is recognized that both combustion and the rusting of metal are oxidation processes.) Stahl believed that the rust was the substance left behind as the phlogiston in a metal was consumed. The contradiction here was that metals actually gain mass (as evidenced by an increase in weight) when they rust. Stahl and other chemists were apparently willing to overlook this paradox because the gain in mass was quite small, too small, they believed, to be significant.

It is the apparently insignificant paradoxes and inconsistencies that modern scientists pounce on, seeking to explain. Lavoisier burned various substances in enclosed containers. He found that the weight of the enclosed substance after burning was greater than its weight before burning. Lavoisier reasoned that if the substance remaining after burning was heavier than the substance before burning, it must have gained its weight from something. The only "something" in the enclosed container was air. Lavoisier further reasoned that if, in fact, the burned substance gained weight from the surrounding air, a partial vacuum must be produced in the enclosed container. This he proved simply by opening the container and hearing the air rush in. Furthermore, when he weighed everything after the container had been opened, he discovered that the weight of the air that had entered the container was equal to the weight gained by the substance that had been burned.

These experiments, painstakingly measured, disproved the phlogiston theory. Combustion was not the loss of phlogiston, but, rather, the *combination* of the burning (or rusting) substance with some element of the air. In the process of beginning to explain combustion, Lavoisier laid the groundwork for modern chemistry, which is founded in precise measurement and the significance of precise measurement.

Conservation of Mass, 1789

In 1789, Lavoisier published the fruits of a lifetime devoted to chemistry, a major textbook. His devotion to precise measurement had led him to confirm by observation one of the cardinal tenets of chemistry and one of the great discoveries of physical science, the law of conservation of mass. In any closed system, Lavoisier wrote, the total amount of mass remained the same, regardless of what physical or chemical processes were at work. In short, matter is neither created nor destroyed, merely transformed. In any closed system, provided that measurements are made precisely, what goes into one substance must come out of another.

1779

Jan Ingenhousz Discovers Photosynthesis

In 1771, the British chemist Joseph Priestley was curious about a possible connection between the fact that carbon dioxide supported neither combustion nor life. At least, that was the common conclusion, and, certainly, animals died if they were shut up in a container in which the oxygen had been replaced by carbon dioxide. To check if this principle held true for *all* life, Priestley tested a plant. He lit a candle and lowered a bell jar over it. When the candle guttered out, he knew that the oxygen had been consumed and replaced by carbon dioxide. Priestley quickly placed a glass of water containing a sprig of mint into this carbon dioxide environment. He expected that it would soon die. In fact, the specimen flourished.

That was a surprise. But there was even more. When Priestley placed a mouse into this environment, expecting that it would die, it survived very nicely. Clearly, the plant had somehow restored breathable elements to the environment. It had converted the carbon dioxide into oxygen.

Eight years later, a curious Dutch physician, Jan Ingenhousz, reading of Priestley's remarkable result, wanted to see it for himself. Scientists routinely repeat the experiments of others, in part to confirm the result, in part to see if they can add to the original observations, and in part to introduce new variations to the experiment. Ingenhousz repeated Priestley's procedure, but added a crucial element to the experiment. He found that the conversion of carbon dioxide to oxygen took place only in the presence of sunlight. A plant left in the dark behaved exactly as an animal did: It consumed oxygen and produced carbon dioxide. Although Ingenhousz didn't come up with a name for this process, he had discovered photosynthesis, one of the most basic processes of life and the key to the ecological relationship between plants and animals.

1783

The Montgolfier Brothers Devise a Hot-Air Balloon

Joseph-Michel Montgolfier and his brother Jacques-Étienne, French paper manufacturers, became interested in a common phenomenon: the fact that warm air rises. They reasoned that if they could trap warm air in a bag made of light paper—put, as they lyrically said, "clouds into bags"—the bag would rise. On a small scale, this worked very well. Air heated in a small bag buoyed the bag to the ceiling. But on a larger scale, the brothers had no luck. One of them realized that it was very difficult to get *dry* warm air into a large bag. Most likely, by the time a sufficient volume of damp hot air was inside the bag, the paper would become sodden and, therefore, too heavy to rise. How to solve this? One of the Montgolfiers noticed that smoke always billowed upward from the chimney of their factory. What if hot smoke were put into a large paper bag?

The bag floated.

With their basic problem solved, the Montgolfiers perfected bigger and bigger bags, some made of silk lined with paper. By the time they announced a public demonstration, they had produced a 24,000-cubic-foot globe of buttoned linen lined with paper. They called this a *ballon*.

Suspending the *ballon* over a large fire in the marketplace of their hometown, Annonay, they freed it. It soared 6,000 feet high and traveled more than a mile before landing.

Two years later, in June 1782, the French Academy of Sciences decided it could improve upon the Mongolfiers' achievement. Academicians had taken samples of the heated air, the so-called "Montgolfier gas," within the balloon. They determined that this hot air weighed about half as much as cool air. The academicians were aware that, in 1766, the British amateur scientist Henry Cavendish had isolated a gas of extreme lightness he called hydrogen, and that, subsequently, a Scottish chemist, Joseph Black, had speculated that if a bladder could be filled with hydrogen and both the bladder and the gas weighed less than the air they displaced, the bladder would rise. In fact, the academicians knew that hydrogen was not half the weight of air, but that it was *forty times* lighter. They reasoned that a balloon filled with hydrogen would rise higher and fly farther than one filled with hot air.

The French Academy assigned one of their number, Jacques Charles, to come up with a method of producing a large volume of hydrogen. While Charles worked on this problem, two brothers— known to history only by their last name, Robert—were commissioned to build a balloon made of silk rendered airtight by impregnation with rubber. The balloon, christened the *Charlière*, was ready ten weeks later. It was inflated by holding it over the device Charles had invented: a series of lead boxes filled with iron filings over which the chemist poured diluted sulfuric acid. The action of the acid on the iron produced a massive volume of hydrogen.

Once inflated to a diameter of thirteen feet, the *Charlière* was ceremoniously escorted to the Champs de Mars in Paris. A spectacular crowd of some 300,000 witnessed the ascent of the balloon, which reached approximately 20,000 feet before it exploded and fell to earth near Gonesse, about fifteen miles from the Champs de Mars, creating great terror among the villagers. (A pair of local monks informed the people that it was the skin of a "monstrous animal," which they attacked with stones, pitchforks, and flails. Then the village curate sprinkled the burst balloon with holy water—just to be safe. The villagers tied the remains of the slain *Charlière* to a horse and dragged it in triumph.)

In response to the French Academy's project, the Montgolfiers decided to take the ultimate step and launch a man into the sky. In September 1783, with Louis XVI, Marie Antoinette, and the court of Versailles watching, they sent a sheep, a rooster, and a duck up in their hot-air balloon, to see if living, breathing creatures could survive in the atmosphere aboveground. All three animals made it. Next, an intrepid young physician named Pilâtre de Rozier persuaded the brothers to let him be the first human aeronaut. He and the Montgolfiers experimented with tethered flights; then, on November 21, 1783, in company with a dashing French infantry major, the Marquis d'Arlandes, Rozier undertook the first free flight in a balloon.

No less a dignitary than Benjamin Franklin, resident in France throughout the American Revolution as the special envoy of the United States, was among those who witnessed the twenty-five-minute, five-mile flight above the rooftops of Paris.

Ten days after this, Professor Charles and one of the Robert brothers flew for two hours and over twenty-seven miles, not in a hot-air balloon, but in one filled with hydrogen. Immediately after this flight, Charles decided to go aloft alone. Without the added weight of a second passenger, however, the balloon shot up to ten thousand feet so fast that the terrified Charles barely managed to scrawl a few observations: The air was punishingly cold, and his ears ached terribly—but the great altitude gave him the thrill of watching two sunsets in a single day.

"Nothing," he wrote later, "can approach the joy that possessed me." But he never flew again.

1785

William Herschel Formulates the Concept of a Galaxy

B ritain's foremost astronomer, William Herschel, was well aware that other astronomers had speculated that the earth and the solar system were parts of a much vaster structure, a galaxy, which some had even theorized was lenticular, or lens-shaped.

It was an interesting speculation, but how could it be supported by actual observation, given the vastness of the objects involved?

Herschel was one of the greatest observational astronomers in history. He decided that the only way objectively to determine the shape of the galaxy was to count stars. Gazing with a telescope into the night sky during an era before hundreds of thousands of artificial lights obscured the heavens presented an array of stars far beyond anyone's capacity to count. Herschel, therefore, invented statistical astronomy. He divided the sky into 638 regions distributed across the entire visible hemisphere. Then he concentrated on carefully counting stars within these regions. In this way, he developed a thorough picture of the statistical distribution of stars.

He found that the number of stars per region steadily rose as one neared the Milky Way. At the plane of the Milky Way, the number was at its maximum. In the direction of right angles to the plane, it was at its minimum. This distribution could be explained if one imagined the shape of the galaxy as that of a giant lens, the Milky Way demarcating the longest diameter of the lens all the way around. How many stars were in this lens-shaped galaxy? Herschel estimated one hundred million—a staggeringly large number, which proved to be a gross underestimation. Nevertheless, Herschel was the first to image the larger structures of the universe, and the first to use actual observation to give spatial dimension to the concept of a galaxy.

1789

Martin Heinrich Klaproth Discovers Uranium

The German chemist Martin Heinrich Klaproth had a great interest in discovering new elements. With the Austrian mineralogist Franz Joseph Müller von Reichenstein, he had discovered tellurium in 1782, and he was now fascinated by a mineral known as pitchblende. This black ore contained a yellow substance, which Klaproth identified as a new element. He decided to name it after the newly discovered planet Uranus and called it uranium.

Klaproth's discovery generated moderate excitement in the scientific community, but no one at the time had a clue as to the monumental impact the discovery of uranium would have on the course of history.

1798

Thomas Robert Malthus Formulates a Scientifically and Socially Momentous Theory of Human Population

Through most of history the subject of human population has been treated much like the weather: You can *talk* about it, but you can *do* nothing about it. Common sense made it clear that the population of a given region tended to rise in times of peace and prosperity and fall during war, famine, or disease.

In 1798, the British economist Thomas Malthus made a leap beyond common sense by publishing *Essay on the Principle of Population,* in which he argued that population tended to increase geometrically, whereas the supply of food tended to increase arithmetically. That is, population increased in this fashion—2, 4, 8, 16, and so on—whereas the food supply increased this way—2, 3, 4, 5, and so on. The inescapable conclusion was that the demands of population would always outpace the supply of food, and, therefore, humanity would always be subject to famine and disease, as well as war (the cause of which, Malthus believed, was, at bottom, a struggle over scarce resources).

This outlook was grim, of course. Yet it also suggested that famine, disease, and war were not catastrophic aberrations, but normal and even necessary features of human existence. However, Malthus did not believe that these things were inevitable. He proposed population planning to curb population growth and bring it into line with the food supply. He recommended sexual abstinence and delayed marriage. What he did not foresee is that science and technology would provide some alternatives to his gloomy calculus.

On the supply side, farming, food production, and food distribution methods would be improved, as would the science of medicine. On the population side, birth control without sexual abstinence would become a reality—although one that, for religious, cultural, or economic reasons, is hardly practiced universally, with the result that, in many places on the planet, overpopulation remains a catastrophic problem.

Oral Contraception, 1954

The birth-control pill, an orally ingested hormone that, timed with the menstrual cycle, brings about temporary sterility in women, was developed by Gregory Goodwin Pincus, an American biologist. Years of clinical tests would follow before "the Pill"—as it was popularly called—became generally available. Its cultural effect was momentous, and many historians see oral contraception as the trigger of the "sexual revolution" that revised the mores of the 1960s. Would Malthus have welcomed this alternative to abstinence?

Humphry Davy Discovers Nitrous Oxide, Laying the Foundation for Anesthetic Surgery

In 1800, the British chemist Humphry Davy discovered nitrous oxide. In Davy's day, chemistry was in large part a science of the senses, so the scientist took the potentially hazardous step of sniffing at his new discovery. It made him feel light-headed and giddy, so Davy and others took to calling it "laughing gas." Soon, among elite London society, laughing gas parties became the rage.

But Davy also made another important observation about nitrous oxide intoxication. Under its influence, one felt little or no pain. Immediately, a practical application suggested itself to him. Nitrous oxide could be used as a dental and surgical anesthetic. Dentists began using nitrous oxide within years of Davy's discovery, but surgeons were more reluctant to adopt it. Nevertheless, nitrous oxide was the first chemical anesthetic, and its discovery began to take the terror out of surgical procedures and to open the door to more complex and time-consuming operations, which, without an anesthetic, would not only be unbearable, but impossible.

1800

Herschel Discovers Infrared Radiation

In 1666, Isaac Newton divided white light into its spectrum of colors (see "1666: Isaac Newton Describes the Visible Spectrum"), and in 1800 the British astronomer William Herschel decided to measure the heat produced by the different parts of this spectrum. His question was: Did different colors of light produce different degrees of heat? What he discovered is that not only did different colors produce different levels of heat, but that more heat was produced the closer he moved toward the red end of the spectrum. Just to check his results, Herschel moved his thermometer beyond the red portion of the spectrum—that is, beyond the red, where the light clearly stopped. To his surprise, he found that the temperature rose even higher just beyond the visible red end of the spectrum.

Herschel had discovered that the visible spectrum was not the total spectrum of light, that some light was invisible, and he called the region just below visible red *infrared* ("beneath red"). Herschel concluded that the sun transmitted heat rays as well as light rays. Only later, about half a century after Herschel's initial observations, did it become clear that infrared light behaved just like visible light, except that the human eye did not detect infrared light waves. The invisibility of infrared was a matter of perceptual limitation, and it did not signify that infrared was a "heat ray." It was light, electromagnetic radiation in a part of the spectrum we couldn't see.

Johann Wilhelm Ritter Discovers Ultraviolet Radiation

Just one year after William Herschel discovered infrared radiation (see "1800: Herschel Discovers Infrared Radiation"), the German physicist Johann Wilhelm Ritter began studying the other end of the visible spectrum. As early as 1614, the Italian chemist Angelo Sala observed that exposure to sunlight turned silver nitrate, normally a white substance, dark. Ritter decided to see how different parts of the spectrum would affect silver nitrate. Accordingly, he soaked paper strips in silver nitrate solution and exposed them. He found that the red end of the spectrum had the least pronounced darkening effect, whereas the violet end had the most. Almost certainly inspired by Herschel's experience with infrared radiation, radiation beyond the visible spectrum, Ritter tried exposing a piece of silver nitrate–soaked paper just beyond the visible violet band. He found that the specimen darkened at an even faster rate than the one exposed to the visible violet light. If the portion of the spectrum below visible red was called infrared, that above violet, Ritter decided, should be dubbed *ultraviolet*—beyond violet.

PRELUDE TO MODERN SCIENCE

John Dalton Advances Atomic Theory

Robert Boyle's work with the compression of gases (see "1661: Robert Boyle Lays the Foundation of Modern Chemistry") launched a long period of interest in discovering the atomic nature of matter. The idea of the atom as the elemental unit of all matter was first put forth speculatively by the Greek philosopher Democritus (see "580 B.C.: Thales Conceptualizes the Elements" and "440 B.C.: Democritus Proposes the Atom as the Smallest Particle of Matter"), but empirical evidence for atomic theory was slow in coming.

In 1803, the British chemist John Dalton synthesized all that had been speculated about the atomic nature of matter and, using Democritus's term, *atom,* put forth the atomic theory.

Dalton proposed that matter was made up of indivisible particles, atoms. However, whereas the ancient Greeks had speculated that the differences between different kinds of matter were the result of differences in the shape of the atoms, Dalton brilliantly proposed that the differences were not a function of atomic shape, but atomic weight. This was not guesswork, but the product of careful observation and measurement. Dalton observed, for example, that it takes eight grams of oxygen combined with one gram of hydrogen to produce nine grams of water. He assumed water consisted of one atom of hydrogen and one atom of oxygen. Therefore, an oxygen atom must be eight times as massive as a hydrogen atom. Thus oxygen may be said to have an atomic weight of eight, versus an atomic weight of one for hydrogen.

As it turned out, Dalton's assumption that water was made up of one hydrogen atom and one oxygen atom was wrong (it is made up of two hydrogen atoms and one oxygen), as were the assumptions he used to calculate other atomic weights. Nevertheless, the underlying idea was right on the mark, and a truly useful atomic theory, the key to modern chemistry and a basic understanding of matter, was born.

1809

George Cayley Lays the Foundation for Aerodynamics

I n 1783, the Montgolfier brothers created a hot-air balloon capable of lofting a person into the air (see "1783: The Montgolfier Brothers Ascend in a Hot-Air Balloon"). However, the true dream of flight was to give people the wings of a bird, enabling controlled and powered flight at will. During the Renaissance, the great artist and inventor Leonardo da Vinci drew up fanciful designs for human wings and flying machines, but it wasn't until 1809 that an English scientist, George Cayley, carefully designed genuine flying machines, complete with most of the parts essential to modern aircraft: fixed wings with moveable control surfaces, a tail system, and various mechanisms for propulsion.

The technology of Cayley's time did not enable him to realize his designs in a working aircraft, but, nevertheless, he had laid the foundation for the scientific study and development of flight: aerodynamics.

1818

Jöns Jakob Berzelius Establishes the First Reliable Table of Atomic Weights

I n 1803, the British chemist John Dalton formulated the break-through theory that atoms were the basis of all matter and that differences among matter were not due to variations in shape among the atoms, but were the product of atomic weight (see "1803: John Dalton Advances Atomic Theory"). Dalton took a stab at calculating the atomic weight of various elements, but the tables he produced were based on many erroneous assumptions. Other chemists, excited by the atomic theory, also attempted to calculate atomic weights, and one of these, the Swedish chemist Jöns Jakob Berzelius, spent many years in the meticulous analysis of more than 2,000 substances. The result was the first reasonably reliable table of atomic weights. Berzelius supplemented this data with calculations of molecular weights of many common compounds.

1820

Hans Christian Ørsted Demonstrates Electromagnetism

Hans Christian Ørsted, a Danish professor of physics, demonstrated what many scientists had long expected: a strong relationship between the phenomena of electricity and the phenomena of magnetism. The intuition that the two sets of phenomena were related was based on the fact that both magnetism and electricity involved opposites: north and south poles in the case of magnetism, and positive and negative charges in the case of electricity. Moreover, the opposites behaved similarly in both electricity and magnetism: Opposites attracted one another, and like charges or orientations repelled one another. Additionally, in both cases, the force of the attraction or repulsion diminished in proportion to the square of the distance separating the source of the charges or the two magnetic poles.

Ørsted created a practical demonstration in which he brought a compass near a wire through which an electric current was passed. As the compass neared the wire, its needle pointed at a right angle to the wire. If the direction of the current was reversed, the compass needle swung 180 degrees around, pointing in the opposite direction, although still oriented at a right angle to the wire.

Interestingly, Ørsted did not feel moved to pursue the full implications of his demonstration. It was left to other scientists, most notably the Frenchman André-Marie Ampère, to make the further observations that clearly established the field of electromagnetism as one of the cornerstones of modern physics.

1821

Michael Faraday Demonstrates That Electrical Forces Can Produce Motion, Thereby Laying the Foundation for Field Theory

The British physicist Michael Faraday, one of the great experimenters of science, tirelessly pursued the implications of the exciting new area of electromagnetism. In 1821, he set up an experiment with two electrical circuits and two magnets. In one circuit, the electric wire was fixed near a movable magnet. In the other circuit, the wire was movable and the magnet fixed. When the circuits were energized, the movable magnet revolved around the fixed wire, and the movable wire revolved around the fixed magnet.

The most immediate conclusion Faraday drew from this was that electricity could produce motion—a discovery that would have tremendous practical application in electric motors and like devices. But Faraday went beyond the immediate and practical. He concluded that magnetism is a field, a field that extends from its point of origin, weakening with distance. Moreover, Faraday reasoned, it is possible to chart this field by drawing imaginary lines that connect all points of equal magnetic intensity. Thus the field could be delineated as "lines of force."

Faraday's early formulation of a field theory provided an important foundation of modern physics, which pictures the universe itself as a set of fields, each originating in particles of matter. Faraday's experiment and the conclusions he drew from it provided an early window into the structure of the universe.

1822

Charles Babbage and Lady Ada Lovelace Begin to Develop the First Modern Computer

By the nineteenth century, calculating machines were hardly new. In ancient times, the abacus appeared (see sidebar: "The Abacus, About 500 B.C."), and the mathematicians Blaise Pascal and Gottfried Wilhelm Leibniz had, independently, created more complex mechanical calculators in 1642 and 1693, respectively. In a sense, all of these devices were computers—but only in a sense, and certainly not in the full modern sense. A computer is not a calculator—although it can be used as one—but a machine that can be programmed at will to perform many different tasks based on logic and calculation. Working with another brilliant mathematician, Lady Ada Lovelace, the British mathematician Charles Babbage began to design a machine that could perform varied and highly complex tasks by means of actual programming—the instructions supplied on punched cards. This idea had come to Babbage from his observation of how a Jacquard loom works. It creates complex weave patterns in cloth by following instructions punched into cards. Babbage and Lovelace even went beyond the notion of programming, proposing a machine that could store information and partial answers to problems and that could even print out the results of calculations.

Babbage and Lovelace began work on this machine in 1822. Babbage carried on the project until the end of his life in 1871, but the machine was never fully completed. His design was severely limited by the technology available in his day. The device he envisioned required monumentally complicated systems of wheels and gears, which could not be made efficient and accurate enough to do the work he wanted the machine to do. What was required was a multitude of electronic switches—but the technology of electronics lay many years in the future, and the Babbage-Lovelace computer remained one of history's greatest incomplete inventions.

1827

Georg Simon Ohm Formulates Ohm's Law, Cornerstone of Electrical Science and Engineering

George Simon Ohm, a German physicist, tackled the problem of calculating the flow of electricity between the two points, positive and negative, of an electric circuit. He experimented with wires of varied gauges (thicknesses) and lengths connected to an electrical source of known strength. What he found was that the quantity of electrical current transmitted through a conductor was inversely proportional to the length of the wire and directly proportional to the cross-sectional area of the wire. This allowed him to define the resistance (opposition to the passing of current) of a given wire. In 1827, he stated his observations in a form that is known as Ohm's Law: "Current through a conductor is directly proportional to the potential difference and is inversely proportional to the resistance." This formulation provides the key for many other calculations, which enable the design of a myriad of practical electric and electronic devices. On Ohm's Law, the science and technology of electrical engineering is built.

1828

Friedrich Wöhler Synthesizes Urea, Thereby Demolishing the Notion That Only Organisms Can Produce Organic Substances

Many scientists agreed that organic substances could be produced only by living organisms, that these substances were the product of some special force or divine essence of life. Theologians and other conservative thinkers were heartened by this view, called vitalism, which seemed to uphold the supernatural sacredness of life. In 1828, however, the German chemist Friedrich Wöhler made an accidental discovery that exploded the vitalist view.

He was heating ammonium cyanate, a garden-variety inorganic substance, and found that, heated, the substance formed crystals that looked to him like urea, the chief constituent of mammalian urine, including human urine. He subjected the crystals to analysis and confirmed that they were indeed urea. The wall between organic and inorganic chemistry dissolved and, with it, the long-cherished notion that life was a divine and supernatural phenomenon.

1831

Faraday Invents the Electric Generator, and Joseph Henry Invents the Electric Motor

L ittle more than a decade after Ørsted demonstrated that electric current creates a magnetic effect (see "1820: Hans Christian Ørsted Demonstrates Electromagnetism"), the great British experimentalist Michael Faraday reasoned that the reverse must also be true: Magnetism could produce electric current.

In 1831, Faraday wound a wire coil around a portion of an iron ring and attached the wires to a battery. When current flowed, a magnetic field was created. He wrapped a second coil around another portion of the ring, connecting these wires to a galvanometer, a compass-like device that indicated the presence of an electric current. When he connected the first coil to the battery, the galvanometer needle jumped—but then returned to a neutral position until the current was removed. The needle then jumped in the opposite direction.

Faraday had discovered electromagnetic induction, the principle behind an electrical transformer. He explained the failure to induce a continuous flow of current by reasoning that, when the current was applied, magnetic lines of force crossed to the second coil, inducing a current. When the current was removed, the lines of force crossed back from the second to the first coil, inducing an electrical current in the opposite direction. However, when the current was applied continuously, equilibrium was reached: No lines of force crossed the second coil in either direction.

Faraday reasoned that there was a technical way to cut across the lines of force in continual fashion. He set up a copper wheel so that its rim passed between the poles of a permanent horseshoe magnet. Wires led from the copper wheel. As long as the wheel was turned, continuously cutting through the lines of magnetic force, an electric current flowed in the wheel. The current produced could be transmitted through the wires to do work. Faraday had invented the generator.

Later the same year, another English scientist, Joseph Henry, inverted Faraday's generator. He reasoned that if rotary motion could produce an electric current, an electric current should be able to produce rotary motion. He improved Faraday's generator, then supplied current to the machine, which, acting on the permanent magnet, forced the wheel to move. The electric motor, in effect the mirror image of the electrical generator, was born. Together, the generator and the motor opened the door to a vast new range of electrically driven technologies and industries.

1833

Anselme Payen Isolates Diastase, the First Enzyme Active Outside of a Living Organism

The French chemist Anselme Payen was a sugar refiner, who managed a factory that extracted sugar from sugar beets. In 1833, he was able to separate from malt extract a substance that catalyzed (accelerated) the conversion of starch to glucose. He called this substance *diastase*, a name derived from the Greek verb meaning to separate, because diastase separated the components of starch into the units of glucose.

Diastase was the first organic catalyst—or enzyme—isolated from the living matter that had produced it. Moreover, it was the first enzyme made active outside of a living organism. It represented a giant leap in the development of organic chemistry and the commercial exploitation of organic chemistry.

Louis-Jacques-Mandé Daguerre Invents Photography

Louis-Jacques-Mandé Daguerre, a French artist, was highly familiar with the camera obscura, a device at least as old as the Renaissance, which projected a focused image on a plane, and which artists had for centuries found highly useful in painting landscapes and other scenes in realistic perspective. Daguerre wanted to take the camera obscura image a step further. Instead of tracing the projected image, he wanted to find a way to fix that image permanently using a chemical process.

Daguerre understood that silver salts darkened upon exposure to light. By focusing an image on a surface coated with a suspension of silver salts, the chemical would be darkened selectively, depending on the intensity of the light falling on any given area. Normally, however, silver salts continued to darken as they were further exposed to light, thereby destroying the image. Daguerre's breakthrough came in 1839 when he discovered that he could bathe the photographic image in sodium thiosulfate solution, which would dissolve whatever silver had not been acted on by the light. Once dissolved and washed away, there was no unexposed silver to darken, and what was left behind was the light-transformed silver, which recorded the image of the light to which it had been exposed. The age of photography had begun.

1842

Christian Johann Doppler Describes the Doppler Effect, a Cornerstone of Modern Astronomy

The distinctive sound of a locomotive whistle—rising in pitch as the train approaches, descending in pitch as it passes and recedes—fascinated people in the early days of the railroads. One person, the Austrian physicist Christian Johann Doppler, decided to dig beneath the fascination. He proposed that the change in pitch was caused by the fact that the sound waves partake of the motion of their source. As the locomotive approaches the listener, the sound waves reach the ear at progressively shorter intervals; therefore, the frequency is higher and so is the pitch. As the locomotive moves away, the sound waves reach a stationary listener at progressively longer intervals, the frequency is lower, and so, of consequence, is the pitch.

Doppler became so intrigued by the mathematics of waves from moving sources that he arranged for a locomotive to pull a flatcar on which trumpet players sounded various notes. Stationed at intervals along the track were musicians with perfect pitch, who were asked to record exactly what note they heard. In this way, Doppler was able to measure the degree of the "Doppler effect" by noting the variation between the note sounded and the note perceived.

The Doppler effect provided important insight into the nature of waves, light (electromagnetic) waves as well as sound waves. In the twentieth century, the American astronomer Harlow Shapley would use the Doppler effect to demonstrate that the universe was not only expanding, but expanding at an accelerating rate. In this insight was the birth of modern cosmology—the science of the birth, structure, and evolution of the universe.

1844

Samuel F. B. Morse Perfects the Telegraph

Samuel F. B. Morse was not trained as a scientist, but as a painter. While returning from a stay in Europe—European credentials were essential to the success of an American painter in those days—Morse met and spoke with fellow passenger Thomas Jackson, a British scientist. The conversations gave Morse the idea that electrical current could be used as a medium for communication.

When he arrived home, Morse did not take up his brushes, but instead designed and built what he called the *telegraph,* a word from two Greek roots, *tele,* meaning distant, and *graph,* signifying writing.

In a scientific journal, Morse read about Hans Christian Ørsted's demonstration of electromagnetism and induction (see "1820: Hans Christian Ørsted Demonstrates Electromagnetism"). Morse wasn't the first to follow up on Ørsted. Several scientists experimented with "deflecting-needle telegraphs," essentially compass needles that moved in response to a current, and William F. Cooke and Charles Wheatstone installed a working deflecting-needle telegraph along an English rail line in 1837. But the device was not practical. Morse decided that electromagnetism rather than mere induction was a more robust technology, and he built his device around an electromagnet. When energized by a current from the line—when the remote operator pressed his "telegraph key"—an electromagnet attracted a soft iron armature, which was designed to make marks on a moving strip of paper. If the telegraph key was held down very briefly, a short mark, or dot, was inscribed. If held down longer, a longer mark, or dash, was produced. Using combinations of these two symbols, dot and dash, Morse created a logical system for encoding the entire alphabet, numbers, and punctuation: the Morse code.

Morse was not only a brilliant practical inventor, he was a highly competent self-promoter, who quickly persuaded Congress to finance a test wire between Washington, D.C., and Baltimore, a distance of about forty miles. On May 24, 1844, he transmitted the first telegraphic message over that wire: "What hath God wrought?" Within ten years, those forty miles of wire grew to 23,000. The age of electromechanical communication was born.

1847

Hermann Ludwig Ferdinand von Helmholtz Formulates the First Law of Thermodynamics (Conservation of Energy)

n 1668, John Wallis formulated the Law of Conservation of Momentum (see "1668: John Wallis Formulates the Law of Conservation of Momentum, First of the Laws of Conservation That Are Fundamental to Our Understanding of the Universe"), and in 1789, the French chemist Lavoisier demonstrated conservation of mass (see sidebar: "Conservation of Mass, 1789"). Some scientists began to speculate that energy might also be subject to conservation: that is, neither be created nor destroyed, but merely transformed. If this were indeed the case, the universe could be conceptualized as an ultimately finite place, in which transformations continually took place, but matter and energy remained constant.

In 1843, the British physicist James Prescott Joule experimentally demonstrated that work—the use of mechanical energy—produced heat. A fixed quantity of work yielded a fixed quantity of heat. (In fact, 41,800,000 ergs of work produce 1 calorie of heat.) This result suggested that energy was indeed conserved; that is, mechanical energy considered "lost" as friction was not lost at all, but merely converted to heat.

Four years after Joule's experiments, the German physicist Hermann Ludwig Ferdinand von Helmholtz synthesized Joule's data with his own and formulated a fully persuasive Law of Conservation of Energy: The energy in the universe is fixed and finite; it is neither created nor destroyed, but is converted from one form to another. Also called the First Law of Thermodynamics, conservation of energy stands as the most basic law of nature in that it describes a fundamental property of the universe.

William Thomson, Baron Kelvin, Conceptualizes Absolute Zero

At the end of the seventeenth century, in 1699, Guillaume Amontons, a French physicist, observed that the volume of a fixed quantity of a gas increases with a rise in temperature and decreases with a fall in temperature. Looking back at this insight a century and a half later, the British physicist William Thomson, Baron Kelvin, realized that the important point was not the obvious one, the loss of volume with temperature reduction, but the loss of energy. He calculated the rate of energy loss to be such that "absolute zero"—a condition without energy—would be attained at −273°C (a figure modern scientists refined to −273.15°C or −459.67°F).

Kelvin suggested that scientists should work from a new temperature scale, one without negative numbers, an absolute scale beginning with absolute zero. Each degree of this new scale would correspond with one Celsius degree, so that water froze not at 0°C but at 273°K (or 273.15°K). (Kelvin himself proposed designating absolute temperatures with the letter "A," for absolute, but later scientists named the unit in Kelvin's honor, abbreviated "K.")

Why was it so important to rethink the temperature scale? The concept of absolute zero signified a state in which atoms are motionless, a state, that is, without energy. Only with atomic movement was energy—heat—generated. Thus absolute temperature was a true measure of energy and, therefore, a supremely useful tool for creating the science of thermodynamics.

1850

Rudolf Julius Emanuel Clausius Formulates the Second Law of Thermodynamics (Entropy)

Conservation of energy, the First Law of Thermodynamics, was formulated in 1847 (see "1847: Hermann Ludwig Ferdinand von Helmholtz Formulates the First Law of Thermodynamics [Conservation of Energy]"). There was something profoundly comforting about this law, which affirmed the ultimate stability of the universe. Although no "new" energy could be created, none of the energy existing in the universe was ever lost.

Yet to anyone who ever did any work or operated any mechanical device, the notion of conservation of energy seemed to have little practical value. In a *universal* sense, energy was not lost, but in a *practical* or *local* sense, it was lost all the time. The French physicist Nicolas-Léonard-Sadi Carnot mathematically demonstrated the unavoidable inefficiency of steam engines, the fact that only a given amount of heat energy could be converted to mechanical energy. The rest, in practical terms, was "lost"—that is, unavailable for conversion. In 1850, Rudolf Julius Emanuel Clausius, a German physicist, generalized Carnot's finding to all energy conversions. Some energy was always "lost" to heat, and heat (as Carnot had demonstrated) could never be converted completely to any other form of energy. Thus, energy conversion was always inherently inefficient.

On the local level, the implication of this is that all machines are doomed to be more or less inefficient. Bad as this is, the implication is far more dire from the universal perspective. While energy is neither created nor destroyed, energy conversion is inefficient and, therefore, the energy of the universe is continually being degraded to heat, which, in turn, can never be fully converted to another form of energy. While the amount of energy in the universe remains constant, the amount of *useful* energy constantly decreases.

This, Clausius argued, could be demonstrated in a closed system. The ratio of the heat content of such a system would always increase during any process within the system. Clausius called this ratio—of heat content to absolute temperature—entropy. It is the heart of the Second Law of Thermodynamics. The amount of entropy in the universe always increases, destined to reach a maximum some day, at which point no useful energy will be left in the universe and, as a consequence, disorder will be literally universal. If the First Law of Thermodynamics signified that the universe was a system of ultimate order, the Second signified precisely the opposite, that it is a system of *ultimate* disorder.

1855

Alexander Parkes Dissolves Pyroxylin in Alcohol, Producing the First Synthetic Plastic

Chemists are inveterate tinkerers, and one of these, the Britisher Alexander Parkes, working with a partly nitrated cellulose called pyroxylin, discovered that if the substance was dissolved in a solution of alcohol, ether, and camphor, it emerged as a hard solid once the solution had evaporated. Moreover, this solid became soft and malleable when it was heated, then hardened again when cooled.

Parkes was a chemist, neither a businessman nor an inventor. He recorded the pyroxylin episode as a curiosity, but took it no further. In fact, he had created the first synthetic plastic, the material that, during the twentieth century, would come to constitute a great deal of the world's built environment.

William Henry Perkin Develops the First Synthetic Dye

Our manufactured world is varied and colorful. We take for granted that we can have paint and clothing in any color we can imagine. But this was not always the case. Through most of the history of civilization, color was a precious commodity. Fabrics were naturally off-white. They could be dyed with a few natural substances, but the resulting array of colors was limited and subject to fading. Many natural dye substances were also rare and costly.

William Henry Perkin, a British student of chemistry, was not thinking about dyes when he ambitiously engaged in a search for a process to synthesize quinine. In nature, quinine, an antimalaria drug, is derived from the bark of a tree. During the nineteenth century, quinine was vitally important to the British empire, which was continually expanding into tropical regions, where malaria was a grim fact of life. If quinine could be synthesized, greatly increased production of the drug would be possible. What Perkin did not realize, however, was that the molecular structure of quinine was far too complex for him to synthesize with the chemical technology of 1856. However, what he did manage to produce, quite by accident, was a purplish substance. Dissolving this in alcohol, he saw that it produced a gorgeous color that would, only later, be christened mauve.

Perkin was a better businessman than chemist, and he immediately saw the potential of the substance as a dyestuff. Once he confirmed that it could be used as a dye, he abandoned his chemistry studies, persuaded his family to invest all they had in setting up a factory, and William Henry Perkin became an enormously wealthy man as the creator and producer of the world's first synthetic dye. While this enriched Perkin, the discovery also opened the door to a dazzling array of synthetic dyes, which not only transformed the manufactured world into a colorful one, but set the stage for all manner of photographic reproduction technologies that would further transform and enrich modern life.

1856

Louis Pasteur Saves the Wine Industry of France with Pasteurization

The chemist Louis Pasteur, a scientist and French patriot, was deeply concerned by a crisis menacing his nation's economically crucial wine industry. During aging, wine was going sour at an alarming rate.

Pasteur investigated wine samples under the microscope and made the remarkable discovery that, in properly aged wine, yeast cells were visible as spherical globules, whereas in souring wine, the cells were oblong. Pasteur concluded that two types of yeast cells existed; the "bad" variety created lactic acid, which soured the wine. There was no way to regulate which type of yeast cell would form in the aging wine; therefore, Pasteur recommended that all yeast cells be killed after fermentation (the creation of alcohol) had taken place but before any lactic acid could be produced. To kill the yeast, he recommended heating the wine to 50°C, then allowing the product to age without yeast. Although conservative wine makers protested, they were willing to give the process a try, and when they discovered that it did not affect the quality of the wine, they adopted it universally. It was referred to as pasteurization.

Pasteurization soon found application in other food-related areas, particularly in the processing of milk, which often carried or supported the growth of disease-producing bacteria. As for Pasteur, the successful experience with the wine industry turned his attention increasingly to the power of microbes—mighty organisms too small even to be seen with the unaided eye.

1859

Charles Darwin Publishes
The Origin of Species

Charles Darwin was not the first naturalist to believe that modern life was the result of a process of evolution, but he was among the first to investigate just what forces propelled and governed evolution. His reading of Malthus's writing on human population (see "1798: Thomas Robert Malthus Formulates a Scientifically and Socially Momentous Theory of Human Population") struck a chord. The tendency to reproduce beyond the capacity of the available food supply was not, Darwin observed, peculiar to humankind, as Malthus thought, but was universal. It was as if nature created a competitive arena in which all living beings vied for survival and mastery. Thus, Darwin concluded, nature dictated conditions in which only the most capable offspring would survive to reproduce. Over time, therefore, traits favorable to survival would be bred into any given species, while those unfavorable to survival would disappear—because animals bearing those traits would die or be killed before reproducing.

Darwin formulated this idea, which he called "natural selection," as early as 1838, but he refrained from publishing it until he felt that he had sufficient observational data to support it. During the course of two decades, Darwin quietly and patiently amassed his data. Even so, it took the appearance of a theory of evolution proposed by another British biologist, Alfred Russel Wallace, to prod the cautious and diffident Darwin into finally publishing, in 1859, his *Origin of Species,* which developed in eloquent detail the theory of evolution by natural selection and thereby delivered to the world a compellingly dynamic picture of life on the planet.

Australopithecus Fossils, 1924

Darwin based his theory of evolution on the observation of living organisms, and he said very little about the evolution of humankind. The twentieth century would see an explosion in the study of fossil of evidence and major discoveries in human evolution. In 1924, Raymond Arthur Dart, an Australian-born South African anthropologist, came upon a fossilized skull in a South African stone quarry. He called it *Australopithecus,* meaning southern ape, but, in fact, it was a hominid, an ancestor of modern humankind, which had lived in Africa from the early Pliocene Epoch (beginning about 5.3 million years ago) to the start of the Pleistocene (some 1.6 million years ago). Today, most scientists classify Australopithecus as the earliest of the hominids and consider it the earliest form of humankind.

Pasteur Advances
the Germ Theory of Disease

The French scientist Louis Pasteur, who had used microscopic analysis to rescue the French wine industry (see "1856: Louis Pasteur Saves the Wine Industry of France with Pasteurization"), was well persuaded of the existence and power of microorganisms. He was not alone. The most radical of mid-nineteenth-century biologists were already theorizing that microorganisms were responsible for causing many diseases, that they were, in effect, the "germs" from which much illness grew.

In 1862, Pasteur reviewed the state of research on the germ theory of disease and concluded that the theory was, indeed, valid. He published a seminal review and synthesis of all the evidence that had been gathered by others in support of the theory, and he lent this material the very considerable weight of his reputation.

Backed by Pasteur, the germ theory gained wide acceptance and motivated many scientists, including Pasteur himself, to set about identifying specific microorganisms as the cause of specific diseases. In this research, medicine entered its modern phase, approaching a time when physicians could, at long last, offer something more than well-meaning support to their patients. The germ theory identified an enemy in the war against disease.

1865

In a Dream, Friedrich August Kekule von Stradonitz Visualizes the Molecular Structure of Benzene, Thereby Providing the Basis for Organic Chemistry

Science aims at the highest application of rational thought. Yet science is an intensely creative field of endeavor, and scientists learn to take their inspiration from wherever it comes, whether as a result of careful calculation or something very different.

In 1865, the German chemist Friedrich August Kekule von Stradonitz wrestled with what seemed an intractable problem. He could not understand—much less explain formulaically—how the important organic compound benzene behaved. How did the molecular structure of this molecule account for its properties? The benzene molecule has six carbon atoms and six hydrogen atoms. This defied chemical logic, as Kekule understood it, because there should be no way of combining six carbon and six hydrogen atoms without producing a highly unstable compound. Benzene, however, was eminently stable. How did this happen?

Exhausted by thought, Kekule was riding in a horse-drawn omnibus and began to doze. Suddenly, he found himself in the midst of a dream. He saw a snake engulf the tail of another snake in its mouth, and the first snake, in turn, take the tail of the second in *its* mouth. In this way, the snakes formed a ring, which began to spin.

Suddenly, Kekule awoke. He saw it all before him: The six carbon atoms of benzene formed a ring (actually, as Kekule conceptualized it, a hexagon); if each individual carbon atom were attached to a hydrogen atom, the result, in this molecular configuration, would be a stable compound. Kekule had visualized the first organic molecule, and on this structural foundation, many other organic molecules could be visualized. Organic chemistry was born.

Gregor Johann Mendel Creates the Science of Genetics

Gregor Mendel was an obscure Augustinian monk and amateur botanist living in a remote Austrian monastery, far from the mainstream of nineteenth-century scientific thought. Curious about the mechanisms of inheritance, the subject that would become known as genetics, he experimented with pea plants in the garden of his monastery. Working alone and with the infinite care and patience befitting a monk as well as a scientist, Mendel made a series of extraordinary observations.

He noted that dwarf pea plants grew from seeds that had been produced by dwarf plants. These dwarf plants, in turn, yielded seeds that also produced dwarf pea plants. However, in the case of tall plants, some produced seeds that always grew into tall plants, while others produced tall plants 75 percent of the time and dwarf plants 25 percent of the time. When Mendel crossed a dwarf plant with a tall plant that always produced tall plants, the result was a tall plant. In effect, the dwarf trait seemed to have been suppressed. But not entirely. For when Mendel took the tall plants produced by a cross between tall and dwarf plants and allowed them to self-pollinate, they produced 75 percent tall plants and 25 percent dwarfs. Mendel thus identified the trait for tallness as "dominant," while that for dwarfness was "recessive"; it didn't disappear, but was temporarily suppressed.

Mendel expanded his experiments to examine a variety of traits, and he also established that the roles of the female and male in contributing to the inheritance of the offspring were equal. In

1865, after many years of observation, he published a paper in which he laid out a set of principles that formed the foundation of genetics and would be called the "Mendelian laws of inheritance." But that title would not be conferred until more than three decades after the publication, in 1865 and 1869, of Mendel's two research papers. Scientists were slow to recognize the work of an obscure monk. Once they did, however, the modern view of the natural world was dramatically transformed.

James Clerk Maxwell Creates a Set of Equations That Unify the Varied Phenomena of Electricity and Magnetism

Ever since Isaac Newton had formulated a set of equations that tied together the phenomena of gravitation, physicists sought to accomplish the unification of apparently varied physical phenomena. The British physicist James Clerk Maxwell did this for electricity and magnetism, showing that both were manifestations of a single electromagnetic force.

Maxwell produced a set of equations showing that the oscillation of an electric current created an electromagnetic field that radiated from its source at a constant speed. He showed further that this constant was, in fact, the speed of light. From this, Maxwell concluded that light was a form of electromagnetic radiation. Indeed, Maxwell proposed that the nature of any type of electromagnetic radiation was a function solely of wavelength. For example, infrared radiation consisted of waves of longer wavelength than visible red light, which, in turn, was longer than ultraviolet radiation, and so on, across the spectrum. Thus Maxwell applied to what seemed entirely unrelated phenomena the same set of equations, thereby demonstrating the unity of magnetism, electricity, visible light, the infrared, and ultraviolet. After Maxwell, such unification increasingly became both the hallmark and the objective of modern physics.

1869

Dmitry Ivanovich Mendeleyev Creates the Periodic Table of the Elements

The concept of atomic weight had its origin in the work of the English chemist Robert Boyle (see "1661: Robert Boyle Lays the Foundation of Modern Chemistry"), and, at various times, chemists attempted to create an orderly table of elements based on atomic weight. The result was never entirely satisfactory.

At last, in 1869, the Russian chemist Dmitry Ivanovich Mendeleyev had the important insight of using both atomic weight and valence (the number of electrons in an atom's outer shell, electrons which it will lose, add, or share when it reacts with other atoms) as the basis of his table. This resulted in a table with rows ("periods") of varying length, a periodic table of the elements, which was published in 1869.

Not only did the periodic table provide a new picture of the order of the chemical universe, it provided a means by which the discovery of new elements could be predicted, because the arrangement of the known elements left gaps. Based on these gaps, Mendeleyev predicted the properties of elements that, in 1871 (the year he discussed the gaps), had yet to be found.

1870

Heinrich Schliemann Locates the Site of Troy, in Effect Launching the Modern Science of Archaeology

Heinrich Schliemann was a poor German lad who made good, becoming a successful businessman. His lifelong motivation was not wealth for its own sake, but for the funding of a dream that had begun in childhood: an expedition to locate the lost city of Troy, fabled in Homer's *Iliad*.

Schliemann was a scientific amateur. At the time, this would have been true about anyone with Schliemann's interests. In 1870, archaeology did not exist as a professional scientific discipline. But he had devoured the *Iliad*, and, following its description of Troy, he identified precisely the right place in Turkey to begin his dig. He uncovered a trove: one ancient city built atop another. Not only did he prove the existence of Troy, he so thrilled the popular and scientific community that, single-handedly, he launched archaeology as a major field.

1876

Alexander Graham Bell Invents the Telephone

Alexander Graham Bell was a Scots immigrant to the United States, the child of a family of celebrated teachers of speech. As a young man, Bell decided to specialize in teaching the deaf to speak, and in 1872 he opened a school for the deaf in Boston. The following year, he was appointed professor of speech and vocal physiology at Boston University.

It was a noble calling, and Bell was good at it. But his imagination resisted confinement to any one profession. His study of the physiology and physics of speech soon expanded into a more general interest in sound and the recording and transmission of sound. Electricity, in the form of the telegraph, was already well established as a medium for communication (see "1844: Samuel F. B. Morse Perfects the Telegraph"), and Bell reasoned that if he "could make a current of electricity vary in intensity precisely as the air varies in density during the production of sound," he could "transmit speech telegraphically."

The concept was a breakthrough, but the problem remained: Just *how* could sound waves be converted into electrical impulses?

Bell set to work, and by 1876, after two years of experimentation, he had developed a microphone and a speaker. The first converted sound into a weak fluctuating electric current. The second converted that current into physical vibration—sound. Even before he had perfected the twin devices, Bell filed for a patent.

With the patent pending, he was now under increased pressure to turn a set of scientific principles into a device that actually transmitted and received sound. Painstakingly tinkering and adjusting, exhausted, Bell toppled a beaker of battery acid into his lap. The sulfuric acid burned clothes and flesh, and, without thinking about it, Bell called into the instrument on his workbench, summoning his assistant, Thomas Watson, who was stationed at the receiver in another room.

"Mr. Watson, come here. I want you."

They were the first words spoken over a telephone. Fittingly, they were a call for help, the most elemental form of human communication. They were prophetic words, a glimmer of just how indispensable the telephone would become to modern civilization.

Thomas Alva Edison Invents the Phonograph and Records Sound

On the face of it, Thomas Edison showed little intellectual promise as a lad growing up in small-town Michigan. He was a poor student, soon dropping out of grade school to be tutored at home by his devoted mother, and he was partially deaf, the result of a childhood illness compounded by an injury. Initiative he did have, making his way as a "candy butcher," selling candy and newspapers to railroad passengers, earning money to finance his real passion, which was tinkering with chemicals. Fascinated by the telegraph, he became a journeyman railroad telegrapher, and this turned his tinkering to electricity. He made the decision to become an inventor.

After selling a telegraphic stock ticker to a group of Wall Street investors, Edison built a fine workshop and laboratory, first in Newark, New Jersey, and then, on a larger scale, in rural Menlo Park. He turned out inventions with such startling regularity that he was soon dubbed "the wizard of Menlo Park." But he plowed most of the money he made back into his work and, as a result, was chronically strapped for cash. Under the goad of necessity, one summer day in 1877, he rushed to complete the design for a machine that would transcribe telephone messages graphically. To do this, Edison used a stylus-tipped carbon transmitter, which made impressions on a strip of paper impregnated with paraffin. By accident, Edison discovered that, when the paper was pulled back beneath the stylus, the indentations that had been made by the original sounds reproduced those sounds—not well, but at least recognizably.

Edison had the happy faculty of combining accident with insight. He immediately sketched a crude diagram of a device that applied the stylus not to wax paper, but to a cylinder wrapped in tin foil. He handed the sketch to his chief engineer and said, simply, "Build this." He did not bother to explain what it was.

Building it was easy. There was very little to the machine, basically a cylinder attached to a crank. As soon as the machine was ready, Edison bent over a funnel-shaped object attached to a diaphragm, which, in turn, was linked to a stylus touching the cylinder. As he cranked the cylinder, Thomas Edison spoke into the funnel: "Mary had a little lamb. Its fleece was white as snow." Then he stopped talking and moved the stylus to the beginning of what he had recorded. He turned the crank, and the machine played back the nursery rhyme.

Edison had invented the phonograph. More importantly for the history of science and civilization, he had recorded *sound,* that most ephemeral of human products. If the telegraph and telephone annihilated space, Edison's phonograph arrested time by preserving, in grooves of foil and, later, wax, the past.

Edison Invents the Incandescent Electric Light

Thomas Edison, who would come to hold more than one thousand U.S. patents, is best known as the inventor of the electric light. In truth, electricity had been used for illumination since the beginning of the nineteenth century. Arc lamps, which produced a blindingly brilliant continuous spark between two carbon rods, were already used in some searchlights, theatrical lighting, lighthouse beacons, and even street lighting by mid century. What Edison grasped, however, was that arc lighting was of no use indoors, at home, in the office, or in the factory. He understood, as he put it, that the light needed to be "subdivided" to be made useful. And, if a way was found to subdivide it, electric lighting could replace gas lighting, which meant that a whole new industry would be created: the business of generating and selling electricity itself.

So, as Edison set about subdividing light, he understood that his aim was to do no less than transform civilization.

He developed the idea of *incandescence,* that is, causing a material—a filament—to glow by passing an electric current through it. The result would be sustained, safe, controllable, "subdivided" illumination. The practical obstacle to achieving this was the filament. Edison experimented with thousands of materials, including a whisker plucked from the beard of a workshop assistant, all to no avail. At last, on October 21, 1879, he "carbonized cotton" by pulling a piece of thread through lampblack—fine carbon. He put this thread into a glass bulb, pumped the air out to create a vacuum, and ran a current through it. For forty hours, it provided steady, usable, safe illumination.

Edison gave the first public demonstration of his incandescent electric lamp on December 31, 1879. He improved it, using new filament material and a new bulb design, so that it burned much longer. With financing from the nation's foremost venture capitalists, he founded the Edison Electric Light Company and, in 1881, opened the world's first commercial electric generating plant, the Pearl Street Station, in lower Manhattan. Before the century was out, all of the urban United States had been wired for electricity. Light had been subdivided.

1880

Josef Breuer Describes
the "Unconscious Mind"

Josef Breuer, a Viennese physician specializing in psychiatric disorders, was sent a patient he referred to only as Anna O, in deference to doctor-patient confidentiality. She suffered from what was called at the time "hysteria," a cluster of psychosomatic disorders—in her case, mainly sporadic paralysis—and other emotional problems. Breuer's approach to treatment employed hypnosis and, sometimes, just conversation. His idea was that both hypnosis and allowing the patient to talk about feelings and fantasies—to talk freely, without censorship of any kind—exposed a level of thought and feeling normally unavailable to conscious awareness. By verbalizing these "unconscious" thoughts, images, and ideas, they became available to consciousness and could then be discussed. The process of such discussion often improved the patient's condition and sometimes dramatically alleviated psychosomatic "hysterical" symptoms.

Breuer acquired a younger associate, Sigmund Freud, who systematized the notion of the unconscious and founded the single most influential theory of mind in modern times: psychoanalysis.

1885

Carl Friedrich Benz Invents
the Automobile

By the beginning of the nineteenth century, steam had been harnessed to propel ships. By the end of the first third of the century, steam was being used to move locomotives along iron rails. But steam had not proved practical for driving vehicles across trackless land. Such vehicles were possible, but they remained awkward and commercially doomed.

In 1860, a Belgian, Jean-Joseph-Étienne Lenoir, invented an internal-combustion engine, which used a mixture of flammable vapor and air ignited within a closed cylinder to drive a piston. Lenoir even attached his engine to a carriage, which it successfully propelled. Nevertheless, the Lenoir engine was very inefficient, and it wasn't until 1876 that the German engineer Nikolaus August Otto developed a four-stroke internal-combustion engine. It worked like this: During the first stroke, as the piston moved outward, it drew into the cylinder a mixture of flammable vapor and air. During the second stroke, as the piston moved inward, the mixture in the cylinder was compressed. When the maximum degree of compression was reached, a spark was set off, which ignited an explosion. The force of this explosion drove the piston outward, sending it on its third stroke, which was the power stroke—the movement that did the engine's work. As the piston moved inward again—the fourth stroke—exhaust, waste gases, were pushed out, and the cycle began again.

The Otto four-stroke design greatly improved the efficiency of the internal-combustion engine, and once it was mated to an appropriate fuel—gasoline, which consisted of smaller molecules than the more familiar kerosene—it was even more appealing as a source of motive power. Recognizing this, in 1885, the German mechanical engineer Carl Friedrich Benz installed it in a small, steerable three-wheel carriage of his own design. Top speed was just under ten miles per hour, but it ran, ran reliably, and could be maneuvered easily. It was the first true automobile.

Heinrich Wilhelm Gottfried von Waldeyer-Hartz Discovers the Chromosome

By the 1880s, scientists had described the events that accompanied mitosis—cellular reproduction. Among these events was the appearance of short threads of a substance called chromatin. A German anatomist, Heinrich Wilhelm Gottfried von Waldeyer-Hartz, focused on the appearance of these threads and proposed that the bodies be called chromosomes. This served to draw attention to them, although it would be many years before the genetic significance of chromosomes was discovered.

Edison Invents Motion Pictures

The "movies" were not a single invention, but a complex technology of many inventions and innovations. In 1867, the zoetrope appeared in England and the United States. It had thirteen slots and thirteen pictures spinning around in a metal cylinder; by varying the number of pictures as seen through the slots, the movement of a figure could be simulated. Beginning at about this time, the British photographer Eadweard Muybridge developed the zoopraxiscope, which combined sequenced still photographs to create a "moving picture" representing the events of a specific span of seconds.

The single greatest advance in the creation of motion picture technology—the recording of light in motion—came in 1889, and it was produced by the American inventor who had already recorded sound. The American pioneer of photographic technology, George Eastman, had created a flexible film base to replace the existing technology of awkward glass-plate negatives. Edison realized that this flexible film, cut into long strips, could be used to record a great many separate photographs taken at extremely brief intervals. The resulting images could then be moved (pulled along by sprocket wheels engaging sprocket holes perforated into the sides of the film) in front of a light that flashed at an accurately timed rate. Because human visual perception is subject to the phenomenon of persistence of vision, the brain would tend to link, smooth out, and, in effect, fill in the intervals between the flashes of light, so that the succession of images would appear to be naturally continuous and moving.

Edison perfected his movie film in 1889, but it wasn't until

1891 that he patented a movie camera to expose the film sequentially. During 1893–1894, he developed the kinetoscope, a peephole motion picture viewer, "to do for the eye what the phonograph does for the ear."

While he perfected the kinetoscope, Edison built the world's first movie studio in 1893 and, the following year, produced the earliest surviving copyrighted film, *Fred Ott's Sneeze, January 7, 1894*, a motion picture record of one of Edison's engineers sneezing. Within two more years, Edison had made a genuine business out of his invention, creating and distributing movies for exhibition in "nickelodeons." The motion picture industry was launched.

1889

Camillo Golgi and Santiago Ramón y Cajal Prove the Neuron Theory

The German anatomist Heinrich Wilhelm Gottfried von Waldeyer-Hartz, the man who named the chromosome (see "1888: Heinrich Wilhelm Gottfried von Waldeyer-Hartz Discovers the Chromosome"), was also the first scientist to suggest that the nervous system consisted of individual cells, which were characterized by elongated extensions. The extension of one cell approached that of another very closely, without actually touching it. Thus each nerve cell, which Waldeyer-Hartz called a *neuron,* was separate. The German's notion that the nervous system is ultimately composed of many separate neurons was dubbed the neuron theory.

Camillo Golgi, an Italian histologist, built upon Waldeyer-Hartz's observations by using a special stain he had developed, which highlighted the neurons for microscopic study. Golgi focused on the gap between one neuron and the other. This he christened the *synapse.*

Finally, Santiago Ramón y Cajal, a Spanish histologist, refined Golgi's staining technique and used it to study the structure of the neuron in far greater detail. He showed how neurons made up the brain and the spinal cord, thereby providing the fullest elaboration of neuron theory. He and Golgi were jointly awarded the Nobel Prize for medicine and physiology in 1906.

1893

Freud and Breuer Publish *The Psychic Mechanism of Hysterical Phenomena,* Foundation of Modern Psychoanalysis

The Viennese physician Josef Breuer had put forth the concept of an "unconscious" in 1880 (see "1880: Josef Breuer Describes the 'Unconscious Mind'") and was soon joined by a younger colleague, Sigmund Freud, in studying the role of the unconscious mind in mental illness and, ultimately, in everyday life. In the process, the two physicians developed therapeutic techniques for accessing the unconscious, a region of thought ordinarily repressed and unavailable to consciousness. Breuer favored the use of hypnosis. Freud used it as well, but gradually turned to what he called "free association" instead. This was nothing more than encouraging the patient to speak randomly, to talk about whatever came into his or her mind, without any deliberate attempt to order the monologue or to censor or edit it in any way. Soon, Freud found that free association provided remarkable access to the unconscious. The more patients free associated, the less they censored. It was as if their own words caught them off guard—and yet they were aware of what they had said, although it took the analytical guidance of the therapist to assist in the interpretation of the free-associated discourse.

Based on what Freud and Breuer now called the "psychoanalysis" of the unconscious mind, the pair published in 1893 *The Psychic Mechanism of Hysterical Phenomena,* which was the earliest founding document of psychoanalysis, destined to be accepted as the most influential and profound psychological theory of the twentieth century and, perhaps, of all time.

THE ATOM AND
THE AIRPLANE

1895

Wilhelm Conrad Röntgen
Discovers X Rays

T he cathode-ray tube is a device in which electrons are accelerated by high voltage and formed into a beam that can be projected. In 1895, while studying how cathode rays caused various materials to fluoresce, the German physicist Wilhelm Conrad Röntgen noticed that certain substances glowed even after the cathode-ray tube had been turned off. He then observed that some of these materials fluoresced even if they were shielded from the active cathode-ray tube. Both of these observations persuaded Röntgen that radiation was projected from the cathode-ray tube and could excite as well as penetrate matter to some degree. Röntgen did not know what this radiation was, so he dubbed it X rays, "x" being the mathematical symbol for an unknown variable.

The discovery of X rays caused a sensation in the world of physics, because this form of electromagnetic radiation behaved unlike any other. While physicists were intrigued by the theoretical significance of X rays, the public was far more interested in the sensational practical application of the newly discovered ray. Once Röntgen saw that X rays penetrated various materials, he used the phenomenon to image the bones of his own hand. Profound as his discovery was for physics—and he was awarded the first Nobel Prize for physics in 1901—Röntgen had also given the science of medicine one of its most practical and powerful instruments.

Joseph John Thomson Discovers the Electron, the First Subatomic Particle to Be Identified

The cathode-ray tube, which produced X rays (see "1895: Wilhelm Conrad Röntgen Discovers X Rays"), greatly interested physicists, who debated the nature of the rays produced by the tube. Were they truly waves? The fact that they could penetrate various matter argued for this. Or were they particles? In 1895, Jean-Baptiste Perrin, a French physicist, exposed a cylinder to a stream of cathode rays and demonstrated that, gradually, the cylinder became negatively charged. Based on this finding, Perrin concluded that cathode "rays" were actually streams of negatively charged particles.

But what was the nature of these particles?

In 1897, the British physicist Joseph John Thomson demonstrated that the cathode stream could be deflected by an electric field. By studying the degree of deflection, Thomson was able to gain an important insight into the particles. He could mathematically derive the ratio of the electric charge of the cathode-ray particle to its mass. To Thomson's amazement, the ratio was extremely high, which led him to conclude that the mass of the particle had to be vanishingly low, no more than a fraction of the smallest atom, hydrogen. Thomson christened this very low mass particle the *electron,* because he believed that the particle carried the fundamental unit of electric charge (which subsequent observation has indeed shown to be the case). The electron was the first subatomic particle—atomic constituent—identified.

1898

Marie and Pierre Curie Investigate Uranium, Discover Polonium and Radium, and Coin the Term *Radioactivity*

The 1890s saw the rapid development of atomic physics based on the phenomena associated with radioactivity. After Röntgen discovered X rays (see "1895: Wilhelm Conrad Röntgen Discovers X Rays"), the French physicist Antoine-Henri Becquerel pursued the notion that fluorescent substances might emit X rays. What he discovered is that one such substance, potassium uranyl sulfate, emitted radiation capable of fogging photographic film. This prompted the Polish-born French chemist Marie Sktodowska Curie to carry out experiments to measure the radiation of a number of uranium-bearing compounds, including potassium uranyl sulfate. Her measurements proved that the radiation came not from the compounds, but exclusively from the uranium atom. This meant that radiation was an atomic and not a molecular phenomenon.

With her husband, the French chemist Pierre Curie, Marie Curie launched an exhaustive investigation of the radiations produced by uranium. When the pair discovered that thorium, like uranium, a heavy metal, also produced radiation, Marie Curie coined the word *radioactivity* to describe radiation-producing properties of certain elements. She and her husband then set about identifying more radioactive materials. They observed that some uranium ores were more highly radioactive than others, but that these variations were not proportionate to the amount of uranium present. Marie Curie concluded the ores must also contain very small (and, hitherto undiscovered) quantities of other radioactive elements, which had to be much more radioactive than uranium itself. Acting on this insight, she and her husband were able to isolate in July 1898 an element they called polonium (after Marie's native land) and, in December, radium, which was very intensely radioactive. The Curies' discoveries took physics to a new level of understanding and opened the door to the eventual exploitation of atomic energy (see "1901: The Curies Discover the Enormous Energy Potential of Radium, Setting the Stage for the Development of Atomic Energy and Atomic Weaponry").

Karl Landsteiner Identifies the Basic Human Blood Types

At least as early as the 1700s, physicians reasoned that withdrawing blood from a desperately ill patient and replacing it with blood from a healthy person (or, sometimes, even an animal) might bring about a cure. In practice, the results were extremely varied and unreliable. While it was true that such transfusions sometimes dramatically improved the patient's condition, it was also true that, very often, the transfusion brought about almost immediate death. Not surprisingly, the practice of blood transfusion fell into disrepute, and, by the mid nineteenth century, was almost never attempted.

At the turn of the nineteenth century, the Austrian physician Karl Landsteiner undertook an extensive study of the nature of blood. He discovered that plasma (the liquid fraction of blood) from one donor would cause the blood of some recipients to clump up. This clumping would block blood vessels and bring about death. However, that same plasma would cause no clumping in other recipients.

Landsteiner set about classifying blood "types," so that physicians could match a compatible donor and recipient in order to save lives with transfusions instead of cause death with them. He discovered that human blood could be classified into four broad groups, which he called O, A, B, and AB. Transfusing blood from a donor of one type into a recipient of the same type was almost always completely safe; however, in a pinch, it was also reasonably safe to transfuse type O blood into any recipient. Type A blood could go only to a type A or a type AB recipient, and type B blood only to a type B or type AB recipient. AB donors could give blood safely only to AB receivers.

Landsteiner's discovery was a medical triumph, which made lifesaving blood transfusions safe and practical. The discovery also had a side benefit for the field of forensics. Now criminal investigators could analyze bloodstains found at the scene of a crime and determine the blood type, which might therefore enable easier identification of a victim or a perpetrator. Landsteiner received a Nobel Prize in 1930.

Max Planck Formulates Quantum Theory

As far as most scientists were concerned, Sir Isaac Newton had nailed just about all of the basic laws of physics by the end of the seventeenth century. For example: Newton viewed light as a product (radiation) produced by energy. Heat an object, and its atoms vibrate—become more energetic—thereby producing light. In terms of Newtonian physics, the more you heat a thing, the faster its atoms vibrate, and the light radiated would accordingly rise in frequency, from red, to orange, and on up through the spectrum into the far ultraviolet.

One problem: This did not happen.

The light radiated from heated objects did not move toward the ultraviolet. Because Newtonian physics seemed to break down when applied to this apparently simple phenomenon, physicists called it the "ultraviolet catastrophe." It cried out for an explanation.

The German physicist Max Planck confronted the ultraviolet catastrophe head-on—until it dawned on him: Energy was not radiated continuously, but in discrete chunks or packets. The size of each "packet" of energy was, in fact, fixed. It was inversely proportional to the wavelength of the radiation in question. Since the wavelength of violet light is half that of red light, the energy packet for violet light "contains" twice as much energy as that for red light.

Planck called each energy packet a *quantum* (the Latin word for "how much?"), and he worked out the relationship between energy and wavelength using a vanishingly small number, 6.6×10^{-27} erg-seconds. This number represented the "graininess" of energy; that is, the only permitted energies in the universe are whole number multiples of this number (which scientists soon dubbed "Planck's constant") multiplied by frequency.

Quantum theory changed our perception of the world—sort of. In everyday terms, for most of us, Planck's constant and quantum theory are of little practical use. That is, on a large scale, the macro scale, the scale we can see and feel, energy does appear to behave as if it were radiated continuously, just as Newtonian physics assumes it is. Only when we penetrate to the micro scale, the scale of the atom, does the quantum "graininess" of energy become apparent.

Even Planck himself did not take quantum theory very far. Its greater implications would be explored by Einstein a few years later in the century (see "1905: Albert Einstein Resolves the Argument Over Whether Light Consists of Waves or Particles").

1901

The Curies Discover the Enormous Energy Potential of Radium, Setting the Stage for the Development of Atomic Energy and Atomic Weaponry

aving discovered radium (see "1898: Marie and Pierre Curie Investigate Uranium, Discover Polonium and Radium, and Coin the Term *Radioactivity*"), the Curies next explored its prodigious energy potential. Pierre Curie found that radium produced 140 calories per gram per hour and did so, it seemed, without diminution. (Actually, the radiation did diminish—but very gradually. The concept of radioactive half-life, which measured the decay of radioactivity over time, was developed later. In the case of radium, the energy output was found to diminish by 50 percent only after 1,600 years.) It was clear to the Curies that the energy produced by radioactive radium was far beyond what any conventional chemical reaction could generate. The Curies' work provided compelling insight into a new universe of energy.

Guglielmo Marconi Demonstrates Radio

In 1888, the German physicist Heinrich Hertz described long-wave electromagnetic radiation, the totally invisible and, to the human senses, imperceptible energy waves that would later be called radio waves. Following up on this discovery, other experimenters explored mechanisms by which radio waves might be used to transmit information—to take the place of the wires that tethered the telegraph to the ground.

One of the experimenters was an Italian named Guglielmo Marconi, who focused on creating a practical transmitter and a receiver (which he called a "coherer"). After working on the problem during the 1890s, Marconi was persuaded that radio waves did offer an opportunity for the creation of a revolutionary system of communication. In Italy, however, he found no one willing to finance his research; therefore, in 1896, he went to London, where he secured assistance from Sir William Preece, chief engineer of the royal post office.

By 1899, Marconi created a transmitter capable of generating a reasonably powerful signal, and in September he equipped two American ships with transmitters to broadcast to receivers in New York newspaper offices the progress of the America's Cup yacht race. This demonstration created sufficient stir to bring meaningful financial investment.

Marconi next decided to send a message across the Atlantic. A number of prominent mathematicians predicted that the effort was doomed. Radio waves, like any other form of electromagnetic radiation—visible light, for instance—travel along the line of sight. The earth, of course, is curved; therefore, some claimed, any radio message would get no farther than the horizon before it traveled out on an unrecoverable tangent into space. Marconi countered this position by arguing that radio waves would conform to the curvature of the earth because of the earth's magnetic field and certain reflective properties of the atmosphere.

On December 12, 1901, he attached an antenna cable to a balloon, which he lofted high into the air. At the other end of the antenna was a radio transmitter fitted with a telegraph key. Marconi tapped out a Morse code signal from his location at the southeastern tip of England. It was instantly picked up by the receiver he had stationed across the Atlantic, in Newfoundland. The age of radio—and electronic communications—had dawned.

The Wright Brothers Make the First Successful Sustained Flight in a Heavier-Than-Air Machine

I n 1896, two Dayton, Ohio, bicycle mechanics, Orville and Wilbur Wright, read an account of the death of Otto Lilienthal, a German aviation pioneer killed in the crash of one of his experimental gliders. The fact of Lilienthal's death did not interest the Wrights, but the gliders he designed did, and the pair began devouring every aeronautical book and article they could find. Their object was to perfect glider design and, ultimately, mate it to an internal-combustion engine to achieve powered flight. By 1899, they had completed their first man-carrying biplane kite, and, acting on wind research obtained from the U.S. Weather Service, they decided to test their machine on the beach at Kitty Hawk, North Carolina. When the glider and a subsequent design failed to perform to their satisfaction, however, the Wrights concluded that all published tables of air pressures on curved surfaces were wrong, so they designed and built, in 1901, the world's first wind tunnel to test some 200 different wing designs. Based on the wind tunnel experiments, they drew up the world's first reliable tables of air pressures on curved surfaces. This in itself was a giant stride in aerodynamics, albeit an unglamorous one.

In 1902, the Wrights built a better glider, which they flew and tweaked more than a thousand times. With the aerodynamics determined, they fitted a 170-pound, twelve-horsepower motor of their own design to the 750-pound fabric-and-wood aircraft. On December 17, 1903, the brothers flipped a coin, Orville won the toss—heads—and he assumed his position at the controls, lying on his belly across the bottom wing of the craft.

At Kill Devil Hills, Kitty Hawk, North Carolina, the engine coughed into life, the aircraft raced down a rail track the aviators had laid across the beach, and, for twelve seconds, over a distance of about 120 feet, it flew.

That day, the Wrights made three more flights, Wilbur managing to remain aloft for almost a minute, over a distance of 852 feet. Quietly, the brothers telegraphed their father, who was back in Dayton: "Success. Four flights Thursday morning . . . Inform press. Home Christmas."

Albert Einstein Resolves the Argument Over Whether Light Consists of Waves or Particles

In 1900, Max Planck laid the foundation for quantum theory by demonstrating that energy is not radiated continuously, but in discrete "packets," or quanta, each inversely proportional to the wavelength of the radiation under consideration (see "1900: Max Planck Formulates Quantum Theory"). Two years after Planck's quantum theory, the German physicist Philipp Lenard discovered the photoelectric effect by demonstrating that light falling on certain metals generated electrical activity. This was the result of the emission of electrons from the surface of the metal. Only light of a certain wavelength or shorter could excite emissions from a particular metal. Depending on the metal, light of different wavelengths was necessary to excite electron emission. Moreover, increasing the intensity of light on a metal resulted in the emission of a greater number of electrons, but the energy of the individual electrons remained fixed. If, however, the wavelength of the light were decreased, the fewer electrons emitted had higher energy. If the wavelength were increased, the greater number of electrons had lower energy. The reason for this relationship between wavelength and the energy of the electrons emitted was a mystery.

Then, in 1905, Einstein solved the mystery of the photoelectric effect by applying quantum theory to it. First, he had to challenge both prevailing theories about the nature of light by assuming that light was neither a continuous wave (one theory) *nor* a stream of particles (the other theory), but, rather, consisted of quanta, discrete packets of energy. If this were the case and, as Planck had explained, the energy of each quantum was inversely proportional to the wavelength of the light, then the atoms on the surface of the metal could absorb only intact quanta. Quanta of long wavelength would not furnish sufficient energy to eject an electron from the metal. This was true regardless of the intensity of the light. But, reduce the wavelength, and each quantum would grow larger, reaching a point at which each was sufficiently energetic to eject an electron from the surface of the metal, thereby producing the photoelectric effect. Shorten the wavelength beyond this point, and each electron would be ejected with greater energy and, therefore, greater velocity. Some metals hold electrons more tightly than others; therefore, the "critical wavelength"—the wavelength just short enough to eject electrons—varied from metal to metal.

Explaining the photoelectric effect was a significant accomplishment, but, even more important was the fact that it had been explained by the application of quantum theory. This proved that, despite Planck's own doubts, quantum theory was a real explanation of nature, not just a mathematical device. Most important of all, the explanation resolved the wave versus particle debate over the nature of light. In some respects, quantum theory showed, light behaved as a particle; in other respects, it behaved as a wave. That is, Einstein demonstrated, light had properties of both a particle and a wave. Later physicists would encapsulate both of these properties of light in the concept of the *photon*.

Einstein Formulates the Theory of Special Relativity

B orn in Ulm, Germany, and raised in Munich, Albert Einstein was so slow to speak that his parents feared he was retarded. In school, he was bored, misbehaved, and was expelled. Bridling under strict German habits of thought and discipline, he left his native country in 1901, settled in Switzerland, became a citizen there, and found work not as a physicist and mathematician, which he was trained to be, but as an examiner in the Swiss patent office. That post did give him time to explore a problem that had resulted from the Michelson-Morley experiment, something that had perplexed physicists ever since the experiment had been performed.

In 1881, the German-born American physicist Albert Michelson built an interferometer, a device that split a light beam in two, then brought the two beams back together. His purpose was to measure the earth's "absolute motion"—the motion of the earth against what was assumed to be the substance of space, a "luminiferous ether," believed to be absolutely without motion. The interferometer would split a beam of light at right angles, sending one half in the direction of the earth's motion. That half of the beam should complete its round trip a little later than the other beam. By measuring the width of the difference between the two beams, Michelson reasoned that he could measure the motion of the earth with respect to the absolute, the "ether."

But it didn't work. There was no difference between the beams.

Michelson kept working, and, in 1887, with the American chemist Edward Williams Morley, he refined the experiment sufficiently to conclude that, in fact, the speed of light was apparently the same, regardless of the motion of the light source relative to the observer.

How could this be? The experiment seemed to indicate that either the earth was motionless with respect to the "luminiferous ether," or the earth dragged this substance with it. However, neither of these cases seemed possible.

In 1905, Einstein put his hand to the problem. He started with the assumption Michelson and Morley had arrived at experimentally (though Einstein later claimed to have been unaware of their result): that the only constant in the universe was the speed of light through a vacuum. In this fact, Einstein reasoned, was the answer to the problem. The Michelson-Morley experiment did not work as expected precisely because there is no absolute in the universe other than the speed of light. There is no such thing as absolute motionlessness, and, therefore, no absolute motion. In short, Michelson and Morley's error lay in attempting to measure something that didn't exist.

Then Einstein stepped beyond merely explaining a failed experiment. Taking the fact of the absolute speed of light, he deduced that length contracted and mass increased with velocity, while the rate of time flow decreased. To say that this was revolutionary is to put it weakly. For Einstein held that everything people thought of as absolutes—space, mass, and even time—were not absolute at all, but, rather, relative to the observer's frame of reference within the very dimensions of space, mass, and time. Since relativity was at the heart of his conclusion, Einstein called his formulation a *theory of relativity*—or, more precisely, a special theory of relativity, because it applied only to the "special" instance of objects moving at constant velocity. (Later, Einstein also developed a "general" theory; see "1916: Einstein Advances the General Theory of Relativity, Thereby Establishing the Science of Cosmology.")

The implications of Einstein's special relativity theory forever changed our picture of the universe, instantly removing it from the comfortable realm of our senses and our common sense. We cannot help but think of space, mass, and time as very separate and distinct things. Einstein suddenly linked them all together, making each a variable relative to and dependent on the others.

Einstein Proposes That Mass and Energy Are Equivalent: $E = mc^2$

The most famous—and momentous—mathematical expression to come out of the theory of relativity (see "1905: Einstein Formulates the Theory of Special Relativity") expressed the relationship of equivalence between matter and energy: $E = mc^2$.

The equation demonstrated that matter and energy are not the radically separate entities common sense tells us they are, but are, in fact, readily convertible one to the other. In essence, one may see matter as concentrated energy. A quantity of energy, E, is equal to an amount of mass, m, multiplied by the square of the speed of light, c^2.

This equation was nothing less than a brand-new lens through which to view the universe. But its implications reached far beyond theory.

The speed of light is an extremely large number—about 984,000,000 feet per second. Square that number—that is, multiply it by itself—and you get an enormously larger number. Multiply this huge product by a given quantity of matter, and you arrive at a measure of the amount of energy that would be produced *if* a process could be found to convert matter to energy very, very efficiently. The necessary efficiency would exist on a subatomic level— that is, only if the energy (later called the "strong force") holding together the nucleus of the atom could be liberated by the "splitting" of the atom. In 1907, no such process existed. Before mid century, however, a process would be found—with devastating results that ended the century's second world war.

1907

Paul Ehrlich Develops the First Chemotherapy, Using Trypan Red to Cure Sleeping Sickness

The idea of curing disease with chemicals is very old. When alchemists took time off from the search for a means of changing base metal into gold, they often experimented with curative substances—sometimes with disastrous results. At the beginning of the twentieth century, the German microscopist and bacteriologist Paul Ehrlich reflected on the significance of the earlier work of Walther Flemming, who, in 1882, observed that certain synthetic dyes combined with (and colored) some parts of cells but not others. Ehrlich reasoned that if a chemical could be found to combine with (and kill) disease-causing cells while leaving healthy cells alone, physicians would have what Ehrlich called a "magic bullet" to fight disease.

After much research, Ehrlich, in 1907, identified a dye he called Trypan red, because it combined with the trypanosome, the unicellular organism that, transmitted by the bite of the tsetse fly, caused sleeping sickness. Trypan red had no effect on other cells. It therefore became the magic bullet for sleeping sickness, and it was the first effective chemotherapy agent ever discovered. Ehrlich's achievement was recognized the following year with the Nobel Prize for physiology and medicine.

1907

Ivan Pavlov Describes the Conditioned Response, Establishing the Basis of Behavioral Psychological Theory

The Russian physiologist Ivan Pavlov observed that dogs salivated at the mere sight or smell of food, not just during the actual process of ingestion. He decided to see if he could artificially create a new pattern, by which salivation would be induced by some stimulus totally unrelated to food or digestion. In a series of landmark experiments, Pavlov showed dogs food simultaneously with the sound of a bell. He attached a surgical drain to the dogs' salivary glands, so that he could precisely measure the amount of saliva produced. He discovered that the dog would soon associate the sound of the bell with the sight of the food and would salivate. After a certain number of repetitions of the ringing bell with the sight of the food, the dog could be made to salivate merely at the sound of the bell, in the absence of food. Pavlov called this a "conditioned response," and it was the basis of a new branch of psychology, behaviorism, which introduced new theories of learning and behavioral development in many animals, including human beings.

Building on the Work of Einstein, Hermann Minkowski Formulates a Theory of Space-Time, a Fourth Dimension of Reality

One of the most brilliant thinkers to grapple with the implications of Einstein's Theory of Relativity (see "1905: Einstein Formulates the Theory of Special Relativity") was the Russian-born German mathematician Hermann Minkowski. In a book called *Time and Space,* published in 1907, Minkowski concluded that Einstein's theory made it necessary to expand the view of the universe beyond the traditional three dimensions and add to these the dimension of "space-time." For Minkowski proposed that Einstein's universe did not permit the separate existence of space and time, but required a special fusion of these two dimensions.

In the so-called Minkowski universe, the traditional geometric dimensions apply within any closed system of reference ("inertial reference frame"); however, when the view is expanded to the universe, apparent space and time intervals between events become relative to the velocity of the observer. For this reason, on the universal level, the space-time dimension becomes critically important.

The space-time concept helped Einstein develop his theory of relativity further, to apply it to accelerated motion so that it could account for gravitational interactions. Ultimately, the space-time concept guided modern theories concerning the shape, extent, origin, and fate of the universe.

1908

Fritz Haber Develops a Process for Fixing Atmospheric Nitrogen to Synthesize Ammonia and Nitrates—a Momentous Scientific Discovery That Also Gives His Native Germany the Power to Manufacture the Explosives Needed to Wage Sustained War

Nitrates are essential to two important products: nitrogen fertilizer and high explosives. Early in the twentieth century, Germany, like other European nations, was preparing for what it anticipated would be a war among the major powers of the continent. German military planners realized that the principal source of nitrates was northern Chile. Those planners also understood that the mighty British navy controlled the seas and, therefore, could cut off access to Chilean nitrates at will. A call was put out to patriotic German scientists to find a synthetic alternative to natural nitrates.

Among those who answered the call was the great German chemist Fritz Haber. He realized that nitrates are nothing more than atmospheric nitrogen that has been "fixed"—converted by leguminous plants and deposited into the soil. He therefore searched for an alternative means of fixing atmospheric nitrogen and found that if nitrogen mixed with hydrogen was placed under high pressure in the presence of iron, which served as a catalyst, the resulting product would be ammonia. The process of extracting nitrates from ammonia was well known and therefore was an easy step once the ammonia had been obtained.

The "Haber process" was a great leap forward in the chemistry of synthetics. It did indeed liberate Germany from reliance on Chilean and other sources of natural nitrates. And it thereby enabled Germany to fight World War I without fear of running out of an essential raw ingredient for the manufacture of explosives.

1911

Ernest Rutherford Proposes
the Nuclear Atom

The British physicist Ernest Rutherford spent several years conducting experiments in which he bombarded various objects with alpha particles. His purpose was to learn about the structure of the atom.

Rutherford fired his alpha particles at a wide variety of materials, including an ultrathin sheet of gold, which, at one-fifty-thousandth of an inch, was a barrier only two thousand atoms thick. By studying the images the alpha particles created on a photographic plate, Rutherford was able to determine, roughly, what proportion of alpha particles were able to penetrate the sheet. He found that particles did pass through, yet some proportion of them were significantly deflected. From this, Rutherford concluded that the atom was mostly empty space, but did contain a "nucleus" of relatively dense mass.

After gathering more data, Rutherford proposed the "nuclear atom": a structure with almost all of its mass concentrated in a nucleus, which bore a positive electrical charge, surrounded by enough negatively charged electrons—of far less mass—to neutralize the positive charge of the nucleus and thereby render the atom neutral. The structure of the atom, at least at its most basic, was now understood.

1911

Heike Kamerlingh Onnes Discovers Superconductivity (Electrical Conductivity with Virtually No Resistance) Near Absolute Zero

Heike Kamerlingh Onnes, a Dutch physicist, liquified helium in 1908, achieving temperatures within just four degrees of absolute zero. This opened up a whole new reality to explore, and Kameringh Onnes set about studying the behavior of matter at these temperatures. One property that greatly interested him was electrical conductivity, which, he knew, tended to increase at lower temperatures; that is, matter became less resistant. Kamerlingh Onnes predicted that resistance would drop to zero at absolute zero; however, when he tested mercury, he discovered, to his astonishment, that electrical resistance dropped to zero at $4.2°K$—more than four degrees above absolute zero. He soon found that some other metals behaved similarly at very cold temperatures, their resistance also dropping to zero.

Kamerlingh Onnes called this phenomenon superconductivity. It would take several decades, however, after the field of electronics and computers was well advanced, for practical applications to be found for superconductivity: the creation of supercomputers of prodigious speed and computational power, their circuits unfettered by resistance.

1913

Niels Bohr Uses Quantum Theory to Elucidate the Nature of the Atom

Ernest Rutherford had painted the broad strokes of atomic structure in 1911 (see "1911: Ernest Rutherford Proposes the Nuclear Atom"), but a significant problem remained unresolved. Take the simplest atom, that of hydrogen. As Rutherford pictured it, it consisted of a positively charged nucleus around which a single negatively charged electron orbited. What was wrong with this picture? The orbiting of the electron around the nucleus should result in the production of electromagnetic radiation, which, in turn, would result in energy loss for the electron, so that it would ultimately be attracted to the more massive nucleus and collapse into it.

No such thing happened.

To explain this apparent anomaly, the Danish physicist Niels Bohr applied quantum theory (see "1900: Max Planck Formulates Quantum Theory") to further explain the structure of the atom. Instead of radiating energy continuously, Bohr theorized, the orbiting electron could radiate it only in quanta, discrete packets of energy that were (on an atomic scale) quite large. Thus the electron, when it radiated, would lose a quantum of energy, which would cause it not to spiral down into the nucleus, but, rather, to descend to a lower orbit—an orbit (or shell) nearer the nucleus. Each time it radiated a quantum, the electron would descend to the next lower orbital shell until it reached the lowest one, below which it could not descend, because it could emit no more energy.

If an atom absorbed, rather than radiated, energy, the electron would rise to a higher orbit, stepwise, with each quantum absorbed. If it absorbed sufficient energy, it would break free of its nuclear orbit. The resulting atom would then be an ion, an atomic fragment bearing a positive charge equal to the number of electrons that had departed.

The rise and fall of orbiting electrons did radiate energy, but only in quantum packets; therefore, the radiation produced would be emitted only at certain fixed wavelengths. Moreover, the reverse was also true: The electrons would absorb energy only at those same wavelengths. By determining these wavelengths, Bohr was able to create a picture of the simple hydrogen atom, showing just what electron orbits would yield the wavelengths represented by the spectrum hydrogen produced.

Other physicists would add much more to the "Bohr atom," but it demonstrated the basic relationship between quantum theory and atomic structure, providing a new understanding of matter and energy.

1913

Frederick Soddy Conceptualizes the Isotope

The periodic table of the elements was a great advance in chemistry (see "1869: Dmitry Ivanovich Mendeleyev Creates the Periodic Table of the Elements"), but research into radioactivity, which spanned the late nineteenth and early twentieth centuries, posed a perplexing challenge to the table. Almost fifty new "elements" had been apparently discovered, but the periodic table had no more than a dozen predictive "blanks" to fill. Was the table wrong? Or was it simply invalid for radioactive elements?

The British chemist Frederick Soddy addressed this puzzle. He formulated the radioactive displacement law, which successfully shoehorned multiple elements into the same available space on the periodic table.

According to the radioactive displacement law, when an atom radiates an alpha particle, that particle has a positive charge of two and a mass of four. This causes the atom that has lost the alpha particle to become a different atom, its nuclear charge reduced by two, and its mass reduced by four. When an atom loses a beta particle, negative charge one, the atom, in effect, gains a positive charge—that is, it gains a larger nuclear charge. The loss of the almost massless electron has virtually no impact on the mass of the new atom. As for any gamma rays the atom may emit, this radiation reduces the energy content of the atom, but, because gamma rays lack both charge and mass, the radiation does not affect the essential nature of the atom.

Soddy concluded that these radioactive changes produced substances that were equal in nuclear charge but different in mass; therefore, they were not separate elements, but could occupy the same place in the periodic table. Soddy called these radioactive variants *isotopes*, derived from a Greek word meaning "same place."

1914

Henry H. Dale Isolates Acetylcholine, Key Chemical in the Transmission of Neural Impulses

nvestigating ergotism—a disease caused by eating grain tainted by the ergot fungus and sometimes characterized by gangrene of the extremities, sometimes by severe psychiatric and neurological disorders—the British biologist Henry Hallett Dale isolated acetylcholine from the fungus. He found that this substance could affect certain organs just the way the nerves that governed those organs affected them. Although Dale did not fully appreciate it at the time, he had discovered the key chemical responsible for the transmission of neural impulses across the synapse (physiological gap) separating one neuron from another.

1914

Henry Moseley Develops the Concept of the Atomic Number

The British physicist Henry Moseley improved on the periodic table of the elements (see "1869: Dmitry Ivanovich Mendeleyev Creates the Periodic Table of the Elements") in 1914 by developing the concept of atomic number. In the Mendeleyev periodic table, the elements are arranged in order of increasing atomic weight, which created a problem, because it made it necessary to alter the order of some elements to keep them in their appropriate families. Moseley used the phenomenon of characteristic X rays— the fact that when elements were bombarded by X rays, they emitted X rays of characteristic (and precisely measurable) wavelengths— to demonstrate that characteristic X rays decreased in wavelength in proportion to the weight of the element emitting the X rays. The heavier the element, the shorter the wavelength emitted. The cause of this, Moseley concluded, was the increasing positive charge of a heavier nucleus. Moseley called this positive charge the "atomic number" of the element, and by ordering the elements by their atomic number instead of by their atomic weight, he was able to correct the deficiencies in the original periodic table. This made the table an infallible predictor of how many new elements awaited discovery and exactly where in the table they would occur.

In 1915, the year after Moseley explained the atomic number concept, he was killed in World War I.

1916

Einstein Advances the General Theory of Relativity, Thereby Establishing the Science of Cosmology

I n 1905, Albert Einstein formulated his special theory of relativity, which was "special" in that it applied only to systems moving at a constant velocity relative to each other (see "1905: Albert Einstein Formulates the Theory of Special Relativity"). After years of work, he published, in 1916, his *general* theory of relativity, which extended relativity to systems moving relative to each other at any velocity, however variable.

In order to generalize the special theory, Einstein had to assume that mass derived from measurements of acceleration—inertial mass—was identical to mass derived from measurements of gravitational intensity—gravitational mass. Furthermore, he had to assume that space was curved in the presence of mass, so that gravitation was not a force, but the result of objects in motion following the shortest path in curved space. Thus gravity was not a function of massive objects attracting one another, as Newton had explained, but was a field, in effect the deformation of space itself in the presence of mass. These conclusions necessitated nothing less than equations that implied the nature of the structure of the universe. Therefore, Einstein's general theory of relativity also marked the birth of modern cosmology, the science that seeks to explain the origin, structure, and fate of the universe.

1916

Using Einstein's Relativity Equations, Astronomer Karl Schwarzschild Describes the Black Hole Phenomenon

The German astronomer Karl Schwarzschild eagerly seized upon Einstein's equations supporting the general theory of relativity (see "1916: Einstein Advances the General Theory of Relativity, Thereby Establishing the Science of Cosmology") to arrive at solutions outlining the nature and structure of the universe. He paid particular attention to what happens to the gravitational field in the vicinity of a very massive star that has collapsed so that its mass is concentrated in a point. Ultimately, he calculated what would happen if a star collapsed to the extent that its volume was zero, and its gravitational pull at its surface was without limit. Anything that approached closer than a certain distance from this point—what astronomers now call the "Schwarzschild radius"—would be unable to achieve sufficient velocity to escape the gravitational pull of the collapsed star. That "anything" includes electromagnetic radiation, light. Because light could not escape, there would be no way to know anything about the star; that is, no information could escape from it. Although Schwarzschild himself did not use the term (it was coined years later), the massive collapsed star acted like a "black hole," a bottomless pit from which nothing escaped.

1917

Using Einstein's Relativity Equations, Astronomer Willem de Sitter Calculates That the Universe Is Expanding

Albert Einstein was a genius, but he was not infallible. His equations for the general theory of relativity (see "1916: Einstein Advances the General Theory of Relativity, Thereby Establishing the Science of Cosmology") assumed that the universe was essentially changeless, static. The trouble was that the theory did not imply this, and, in order to make the equations work—that is, to allow them to apply to a static universe—Einstein had to introduce an arbitrary constant.

Willem de Sitter, a Dutch astronomer, decided to find out what would happen if he approached the equations without the "gravitational constant." The result was not a static universe, but one that expanded. Einstein himself pointed to this result as evidence of the need for his constant, since the idea of an expanding universe seemed absurd. Later, when the American astronomer Edwin Hubble observed that the galaxies were receding, thereby confirming that the universe was, in fact, expanding (see "1929: Edwin Hubble Observes the Expanding Universe"), Einstein called his gravitational constant the greatest mistake of his scientific career.

1919

Rutherford Creates the First Nuclear Reaction

The British physicist Ernest Rutherford performed a series of experiments in which he bombarded various gases with alpha particles. With certain gases, such as hydrogen, the bombardment produced scintillations—flashes of light—on a specially coated screen, indicating that it had been struck by an energetic subatomic particle. Rutherford concluded that the brightest scintillations were produced when an alpha particle struck a hydrogen nucleus, propelling a proton into the screen.

When Rutherford bombarded a more complex atom, that of nitrogen, he also saw the scintillations, but the number of these decreased over time. Rutherford concluded that the alpha particles occasionally knocked one of the seven protons out of the nitrogen nucleus, but, after a time, an increasing number of the nitrogen nuclei absorbed the alpha particles—hence the reduction of scintillations. If this was the case, the following should also be true: a nitrogen nucleus, with a charge of +7 (seven protons), loses a proton but absorbs an alpha particle, which has a charge of +2. The net result should be a nucleus with a +8 charge (eight protons), which is an oxygen atom. Thus Rutherford had combined a helium nucleus (a two-proton alpha particle) with a nitrogen nucleus to form a hydrogen nucleus (a single proton) and an oxygen nucleus (eight protons). Rutherford had produced an extraordinary chemical reaction, actually transferring particles inside the atomic nucleus, whereas ordinary chemical reactions involved merely the transfer or sharing (bonding) of electrons. His experiments produced the first artificially induced nuclear reactions.

Frederick Grant Banting Isolates Insulin

By very early in the twentieth century, there was a rudimentary understanding of the function of hormones in the human body. Physicians at this time also began to suspect that diabetes was caused by some deficiency in the pancreas, and some guessed that this organ produced a hormone that controlled carbohydrate metabolism, without which diabetes ensued. It was suggested that structures within the pancreas known as the islets of Langerhans were responsible for producing the hormone, which might be called *insulin,* from the Latin word for island. However, all of this was speculation, because no one had been able to identify the hormone. The problem was that the pancreas itself digested and destroyed any insulin produced before it could be isolated and extracted.

Frederick Grant Banting, a Canadian physician, had read of an experiment in which the pancreatic duct of an experimental animal was tied off, thereby causing a degeneration of the pancreatic tissue. He reasoned that if the pancreas were caused to degenerate, the islets of Langerhans would still produce insulin, but the pancreas would not be able to digest and destroy it; therefore, it could be extracted directly from the degenerated organ.

With a physiologist, Charles Herbert Best, Banting operated on a number of dogs, tying off their pancreases. Once the organ had degenerated, the doctors were, indeed, able to extract insulin, which they used to stop the symptoms of diabetes. Hormone therapy had been discovered.

1926

Max Born, Werner Heisenberg, and Erwin Schrödinger Develop Quantum Mechanics

Making sense of the Bohr atom (see "1913: Niels Bohr Uses Quantum Theory to Elucidate the Nature of the Atom"), the Austrian physicist Erwin Schrödinger concluded, required thinking of the electron, a particle, as behaving like a wave. Schrödinger called this wave mechanics, and it represented an elaboration of the work of the German physicist Werner Heisenberg, who had earlier developed matrix mechanics.

The German physicist Max Born developed matrix and wave mechanics a step further by treating the electron as both a particle and a wave. That is, he developed equations to predict the behavior of an electron as a particle existing at certain points in a "wave packet" or quantum. Collectively, Schrödinger, Heisenberg, and Born developed quantum mechanics, the physics of atomic and subatomic systems and how they interact with radiation, based on observable quantities. Quantum mechanics brought physics down to a scale of almost unimaginable smallness, in which events can no longer be described in terms of classical Newtonian physics, which is exclusively suited to macro scales.

OUTER SPACE,
INNER SPACE,
AND
CYBERSPACE

1926

Robert Goddard Fires
the First Liquid-Fuel Rocket

ocketry was not new in 1926. Armies had been firing small
rockets at one another since the era of medieval China. Nor
was it a new idea to use a rocket to achieve sufficient velocity to escape the earth's gravitational pull; Sir Isaac Newton had
speculated on this in the seventeenth century. But rockets that used
gunpowder as fuel—and all early rockets did—could never achieve
sufficient thrust to go very far, let alone to achieve escape velocity
(the velocity needed to "escape" the earth's gravity), and, equally
important, they required air to support combustion, so they could
not function once they were beyond the earth's atmosphere.

The American physicist Robert H. Goddard, who, as a boy,
dreamed of building a rocket that would loft him to Mars, pondered the problems of thrust and combustion beyond the atmosphere. He decided that a liquid-fueled rocket, running, say, on
gasoline, could develop far more thrust than a solid-fuel rocket.
What is more, if the rocket could carry its own oxidizer (Goddard
decided on liquid oxygen), its fuel could sustain combustion without the presence of an atmosphere.

Goddard built his first liquid-fuel rocket early in 1926 and test
flew it on March 16, from a "launch pad" on property owned by
his aunt. Just four feet long and about half a foot in diameter, it
didn't look like much. Nor did it get very far: perhaps 200 feet in
altitude. But it was the first liquid-fueled rocket, and it represented
a major stride forward in the science and technology of rocketry. In

subsequent experiments, Goddard identified and solved—at least in a basic way—every major problem of liquid-fueled rocketry, including the development of fuel pumps, self-cooling rocket motors, and other devices required for an engine suited to power missile weapons or vehicles to carry human beings into space.

Heisenberg Formulates the Uncertainty Principle

While much of scientific and technological history is the story of how human beings increased their knowledge and power, the tale also has a counterplot in the discovery of certain limitations. Copernicus, for example, took the earth away from the center of the universe. Breuer and Freud demonstrated that human beings have only limited conscious control over their own thoughts and actions.

Then came the German physicist Werner Heisenberg. By way of exploring the implications of quantum mechanics, Heisenberg proposed that there was a finite limit to what can be measured and known, no matter the skill of the observer or the exquisite nature of the instrument used.

Heisenberg postulated that the momentum of a subatomic particle could be determined to an infinite degree of precision. Likewise its position. However, both momentum and position could not be precisely determined at the same time. The more precisely you attempted to determine momentum, the less certain you could be about position, and vice versa. Moreover, the degree of uncertainty in momentum multiplied by the uncertainty in knowledge of position was equal to Planck's constant (see "1900: Max Planck Formulates Quantum Theory"). This equivalence was no coincidence. It meant, according to Heisenberg, that Planck's constant expressed the "graininess" of the universe—the point beyond which one could gain no more information. Think of a photograph. You can magnify its detail to a certain extent, until you no longer see a clear image, but, rather, the grain of the film's emulsion. From this point on, further magnification will reveal no new information—just bigger clumps of grain.

Looked at from one perspective, the uncertainty principle represents the absolute limit of possible knowledge. Looked at a bit differently, it is simply an operating principle of the universe, which explains certain phenomena that otherwise defy human reason and common sense.

Alexander Fleming Discovers Penicillin

Alexander Fleming was a Scottish-born British physician who became keenly interested in bacteriology while working as a military surgeon during World War I and seeing soldiers survive initial wounding only to succumb later to infection. Fleming was determined to identify substances that could kill bacteria without destroying healthy cells. In 1921, he isolated the enzyme lysozyme, a constituent of human tears and mucus, which, he found, attacked many types of bacteria. But he could derive nothing of practical value from it.

He kept working. In 1928, he was culturing experimental staph bacteria in a petri dish when he noticed that one of the cultures had been contaminated by a mold, *Penicillium notatum*. He was about to discard the petri dish in disgust, but, being a scientist, he looked more closely at it, and he saw that surrounding the mold growth was a circle free from bacteria. Something in the mold had killed the staph.

Fleming set about making sense of this laboratory accident. He soon was successful in isolating the substance in the mold that was responsible for killing the bacteria. He called the material penicillin, and further tests demonstrated that it was effective not just against staph, but a wide range of bacteria. Most important of all, it was nontoxic. And so medicine had its first antibiotic, a substance that transformed physicians from observers of disease and providers of often feeble comfort, to scientists armed with a powerful weapon that could actually fight—and defeat—disease.

The First Sulfa Drug, 1935

Fleming discovered the first antibiotic, a substance that stimulates the production of antibodies, which fight disease. A few years later, in 1935, the German biochemist Gerhard Domagk synthesized the most important early antibacterial, a substance that does not stimulate antibodies, but that is directly effective against infection. He discovered that a dye, Prontosil, was, like Trypan red (see "1907: Paul Ehrlich Develops the First Chemotherapy, Using Trypan Red to Cure Sleeping Sickness"), effective to some degree against bacteria. The problem was that Prontosil was a complex chemical, expensive, and difficult to obtain in quantity. Domagk looked for a way to dismantle the big Prontosil molecule and discover the fraction that was antibacterial. He found that sulfanilamide, a constituent of Prontosil, was highly effective against bacteria. This discovery led to the synthesis of a large family of sulfa drugs, which proved effective against a broad range of infections.

1929

John Douglas Cockcroft and Ernest Thomas Sinton Walton Invent the Particle Accelerator (Atom Smasher)

Ernest Rutherford (see "1919: Rutherford Creates the First Nuclear Reaction") and other early nuclear physicists used alpha particles as investigative "bullets" to bombard atoms and to create nuclear reactions. Alpha radiation, however, was not very penetrating, and, therefore, it was quite limited as an investigative tool. Scientists looked for a means of accelerating ordinary nuclear particles, such as protons, and using these to bombard atoms under investigation.

In 1929, the British physicist John Douglas Cockcroft and his Irish colleague, Ernest Thomas Sinton Walton, built a "voltage multiplier," which created very high electrical voltages powerful enough to accelerate protons such that they became more energetic than naturally occurring alpha particles. This was the first device physicists called a particle accelerator and the general public dubbed an "atom smasher."

Cockcroft and Walton shared the 1951 Nobel Prize for having created an instrument valuable in the exploration of the atomic and subatomic realms.

Edwin Hubble Observes the Expanding Universe

The great American astronomer Edwin Hubble, in whose honor the Hubble Space Telescope is named, reviewed the work of Vesto Melvin Slipher and Milton LaSalle Humason, both of whom concluded that the galaxies they observed were receding from us. Hubble reasoned from their observations and his own that the galaxies receded at a rate proportional to their distance from us, a proposition subsequently called Hubble's Law. And he reasoned further that the galaxies were not receding from us, per se, but from any observer anywhere. If one inflated a balloon partway, then drew dots on it, then continued to blow it up, each dot would recede from the others. Take the perspective of any one dot, and the rest of the dots would appear to recede from this point of view.

If the galaxies were the equivalent of dots on a balloon, what was the balloon? The universe itself. Therefore, the explanation of receding galaxies was that the universe itself was expanding. This conclusion reshaped the science of cosmology and validated the equations Einstein originally introduced to support his general theory of relativity (see "1916: Einstein Advances the General Theory of Relativity, Thereby Establishing the Science of Cosmology").

1929

Jean Piaget Formulates a Cogent Theory of Child Development

Jean Piaget, a Swiss national, had been trained as a zoologist, but he made his most important contribution to science as a psychologist, and he took as his subject of study the development of his own children. By carefully observing their development—and, later, the development of others—Piaget formulated the first comprehensive, cogent, and empirically based theory of child development. Essentially, he saw psychological development as an orderly and universal four-stage journey away from egocentricism and toward a recognition of a self defined in relation to the rest of the world.

1930

Paul Adrien Maurice Dirac Proposes the Existence of Antimatter

Paul Adrien Maurice Dirac, a British physicist, pursued the mathematical implications of the theory that electrons behave both as particles and as waves (see "1926: Max Born, Werner Heisenberg, and Erwin Schrödinger Develop Quantum Mechanics"). From his work, he concluded, at first, that electrons and protons (at the time, the only two known subatomic particles) existed in two energy states, positive and negative. He even postulated that electrons and protons were really the same particle in different energy states, positive or negative. However, the mass of the proton was so much greater than that of the electron that this seemed clearly false. Therefore, in 1930, Dirac postulated that both particles, the electron and the proton, were in the positive state, but that each could also exist in a negative state. That is, Dirac predicted the existence of a particle entirely like the positively charged proton, but with a negative charge. The same was true of the negatively charged electron; an antiparticle counterpart existed, identical in every way to the electron, except for a positive charge.

If protons and electrons made up matter, then antiprotons and antielectrons made up antimatter. For this remarkable concept, Dirac (with Erwin Schrödinger) was awarded the Nobel Prize in 1933.

1932

Karl Guthe Jansky Detects Radio Waves from Space, Inaugurating Radio Astronomy

As radio became an increasingly important medium not only for entertainment, but for communications, static—radio interference—became an increasingly serious problem. Bell Laboratories, the research arm of the Bell Telephone Company, put an electrical engineer, Karl Guthe Jansky, in charge of investigating the sources of static. Jansky built a large antenna at Bell Labs' New Jersey facility and used it to sample static. He soon detected a signal from outer space. At first, he assumed that its source was the sun, but after much observation, he concluded, in 1932, that the origin of the radio signal was in the direction of the constellation Sagittarius, the very direction that the astronomer Harlow Shapley had identified as the center of our galaxy, the Milky Way, in 1918.

From this humble beginning—a search for unwanted static—the science of radio astronomy was born. It would not seriously develop until the 1950s, but the idea had been planted: that the radio portion of the electromagnetic spectrum could now be added to the visible light spectrum as a medium through which the heavens might be studied.

Ernst August Friedrich Ruska Builds the First Electron Microscope

The microscope was a titanic advance for science (see "1590: Zacharias Janssen Invents the Microscope" and "1676: Antonie van Leeuwenhoek Perfects the Microscope and Opens to Study the Universe of Microorganisms"), but, no matter how well designed and how exquisitely made, optical microscopes have an important limitation: The degree of acuity—sharpness—with which the smallest objects can be viewed is inversely proportional to the wavelength of the viewing medium. The shorter the wavelength, the greater the acuity and the smaller the object that can be viewed. The longer the wavelength, the less the acuity, which makes it impossible to view extremely tiny objects, such as objects smaller than the smallest living cells.

The German electrical engineer Friedrich Ruska understood that electron waves were of much shorter wavelength than visible light. If a microscope could be designed to use electron waves rather than visible light waves, it could resolve much, much smaller objects with much greater sharpness than a conventional microscope. Ruska set to work to create an electron microscope, producing a working model—quite primitive by today's standards—in 1932. Over the years, the instrument was greatly refined and improved to the degree that viruses can be studied, as can molecules—objects much too small to be resolved by the relatively long wavelengths of visible light.

1935

Konrad Lorenz Establishes the Science of Ethology, the Study of Animal Behavior

Ethology, the science of animal behavior in natural environments, was unknown prior to the work of the German zoologist Konrad Lorenz, who made the breakthrough discovery of "imprinting"—a receptiveness to certain types of learning, which occurred only at specific, critical points in the life of an animal. For instance, chicks learned to follow a moving object very shortly after hatching. Normally, that object was the chicks' mother, but, Lorenz discovered, the chicks would follow any object if it was introduced during the critical imprinting period. Once the critical period was passed, however, imprinting would not occur again, and once imprinting had been accomplished, it continued to shape the animal's behavior, to some measurable degree, lifelong.

Alan Turing Creates Computer Science with the Turing Machine

The origins of the modern computer are many and varied. Important milestones are covered in "The Abacus, About 500 B.C." (sidebar), "1822: Charles Babbage and Lady Ada Lovelace Begin to Develop the First Modern Computer," "1946: John William Mauchly and John P. Eckert, Jr., Design ENIAC, the First Fully Electronic Computer," and "1981: IBM Introduces the Personal Computer." All of these steps in the evolution of an instrument now so central to our lives have one thing in common. They are all inventions, physical devices: machines.

But the "machine" on which computer science is most directly based was not a physical device at all, but a construct of the imagination.

During World War II, the British mathematician Alan Turing was part of a team dedicated to breaking the German master military code, the so-called Enigma cipher. To break this code, Turing used—in part—a concept he had created shortly before the war, in 1936. It was called the "Turing machine," but it was nothing mechanical or electrical. Instead, it was a "thought experiment," an idealized model. Turing imagined a machine consisting of an infinite paper tape on which a kind of "tape head" could read and write information. The tape head included a modifiable control mechanism, which could store directions from a finite set of instructions—that is, a "program." As Turing conceived it, the tape was divided into squares, each of which was either blank or bore one of a finite number of symbols. The tape head could move to, read, write, and erase any single square and could change from one "internal state" to another between one moment and the next, depending on both the internal state of the machine and the condition of the scanned square at a given moment. Once the machine had stopped the process of scanning, writing, and erasing, the result would be a solution to the mathematical query that had been presented to it.

The technology to realize a practical version of the Turing machine did not exist in 1936, but Turing had provided instructions for what to do when it became available. He did no less than outline the theoretical basis of computer science.

Using an Engine Design Patented in 1930 by Frank Whittle, the First Jet Plane Is Flown

In 1930, the British aeronautical engineer Frank Whittle patented a design for a jet engine. It resembled a rocket, in that it burned fuel in such a way as to eject exhaust at extremely high speed, thereby providing thrust. In contrast to the rocket engine, however, the jet is air breathing—its supply of oxidizer, necessary for combustion, is not some onboard chemical, but the atmosphere itself.

A conservative aeronautical community was slow to buy into the Whittle engine and continued instead to rely on piston-powered propeller designs. However, in May 1941, during World War II, British aeronautical engineers experimented with the Whittle engine as a power plant for an aircraft, thereby coming to design and fly the first jet plane. Although it began later, development of jets proceeded more rapidly in Germany, but, even there, jets were developed too late and were produced in insufficient numbers to have significant impact on the outcome of World War II.

Enrico Fermi Conducts the First Sustained Nuclear Chain Reaction

Albert Einstein's $E = mc^2$ equation described the equivalence of energy and matter, showing that the potential energy of matter, locked, as it were, within the "strong force" holding together the atomic nucleus, was tremendous: the product of mass multiplied by an enormous number, the square of the speed of light. However, a single atom is a very small thing, with a tiny mass. Split a single atom, liberate the strong force, and even multiplied by the square of the speed of light, the energy liberated will not be great from the macro perspective. However, in 1939, the Hungarian-born physicist Leo Szilard advanced the possibility that the fission (splitting) of a single atomic nucleus could induce a "chain reaction" in other atoms, the cumulative effect of which would yield amounts of energy unparalleled by any conventional chemical process.

In theory, a chain reaction would work like this: The particles split off from one atomic nucleus would have sufficient energy to split off particles in the nuclei of more atoms, which, in turn, would do the same to yet more.

That was the theory, and it might have remained on the theoretical level for a long time, had it not been for the advent of World War II and the fear, especially among scientists who had fled to America to escape Nazi persecution, that Germany would attempt to develop a fission weapon. At Szilard's urging, Albert Einstein—now living in the United States—wrote a secret letter to President Franklin Roosevelt, warning him of the danger and urging him to begin a project to develop a fission weapon: an atomic bomb.

That was the beginning of the "Manhattan Project," the greatest scientific, engineering, and manufacturing effort ever mounted by any nation. Its purpose was to beat the Germans to the creation of an atomic weapon. The first step toward this goal was to produce in actuality and under controlled conditions the kind of chain reaction Szilard had only theorized. This assignment was given to Enrico Fermi, a young physicist who had fled fascist Italy in 1938 on the heels of the anti-Semitic decree Benito Mussolini had promulgated in obedience to Hitler. Fermi's wife was a Jew.

Fermi oversaw the design and construction of an "atomic pile" reactor in a squash court under the stands of the University of Chicago's Stagg Field. Uranium and uranium oxide were piled up in combination with graphite blocks. Neutrons colliding with the carbon atoms in the graphite would not affect the carbon nuclei, but would bounce off them, giving up energy and moving slowly as a result, thereby increasing the chance that they would react with the uranium 235. By making the atomic pile large, the chances that neutrons would strike the uranium 235 were increased. However, it was essential that the pile be just large enough to achieve "critical mass," sufficient mass to start and sustain the chain reaction, without producing an uncontrolled reaction: an atomic explosion.

Indeed, Fermi and the other scientists recognized the need to control and shut down the reaction, so they inserted cadmium rods into the pile, to moderate the neutron action. When the pile approached critical mass, the rods would be slowly withdrawn, and the number of neutrons produced would increase. When the rods were sufficiently withdrawn so that more neutrons were produced than were being consumed by the cadmium, the pile would "go critical," and the nuclear chain reaction would begin. Fermi understood that if this were allowed to proceed unchecked, an uncontrolled chain reaction would take place—an atomic explosion. How destructive would that be? No one knew. Much of Chicago could be destroyed, or, some theorized, a chain reaction might be set off in the very atoms of the atmosphere, perhaps bringing the world to an end.

The pressures of war compelled the gamble, the gamble that the chain reaction could be produced—and that it could be controlled. So, just before 3:45 in the afternoon of December 2, 1942, Fermi ordered the withdrawal of the cadmium control rods. Geiger counters indicated a large release of energy—a chain reaction under way. At 3:45, the reaction became self-sustaining. When this occurred, Fermi directed that the rods be reinserted. The chain reaction stopped, and Chicago didn't vaporize, but the scientists were now ready to make a bomb.

1944

Oswald Avery Discovers the Genetic Significance of DNA

The Canadian-American bacteriologist Oswald Avery was studying pneumococci, the bacteria responsible for pneumonia. He grew two strains in the laboratory, an "R" strain, which had a rough surface, and an "S" strain, with a smooth surface. The smooth surface was created by a carbohydrate molecule, which, Avery concluded, the "R" strain was genetically incapable of producing. He prepared an extract from the "S" bacteria, which contained genetic material but no actual cells. Using this substance, he was able to convert the "R" strain into the "S" strain, thereby demonstrating that the extract contained some genetic substance that triggered production of the carbohydrate coat.

In an effort to derive the exact nature of this genetic substance, Avery successively purified the "S" extract until he obtained a substance that still effected the conversion of the "R" to the "S" strain. That substance was DNA, deoxyribonucleic acid. The conclusion was inescapable: DNA was the substance that bore the genetic code of any cell. With this identification, the science of genetics made its greatest leap since the work of Gregor Mendel in the mid-nineteenth century (see "1865: Gregor Johann Mendel Creates the Science of Genetics"). Less than a decade later, two other scientists would discover the structure of this all-important molecule (see "1953: Francis Crick and James Watson Postulate the Double-Helix Structure of DNA").

1944

Carl Friedrich von Weizsacker Proposes a New Nebular Hypothesis, Generally Accepted Today as the Most Plausible Explanation for the Origin of the Solar System

In the mid-eighteenth century, the German philosopher Immanuel Kant theorized that the solar system had begun as a nebula. This cloud of gas and dust, which slowly rotated, contracted until it became flattened into a spinning disk that, in various ways, coalesced into the sun and the planets. The French mathematician Pierre-Simon Laplace elaborated on this "nebular hypothesis" later in the century. Appealing as the hypothesis was, it ran up against a serious problem. Most of the angular momentum of the solar system—about 98 percent—was concentrated in the planets, which, however, constituted only one-tenth of 1 percent of the total mass of the solar system. The physics just didn't make sense.

The German astronomer Carl Friedrich von Weizsacker made a fresh approach to the nebular hypothesis by suggesting that the outer layers of the contracting nebula were subject to turbulence, which caused the planets to form in the orbits that were now observed. Weizsacker's modification of the nebular hypothesis is the most widely accepted explanation of the genesis of the solar system.

A Massive American Research Team Led by J. Robert Oppenheimer Develops a Nuclear Fission (Atomic) Bomb

With the theory of the nuclear chain reaction proven in fact by Enrico Fermi (see "1942: Enrico Fermi Conducts the First Sustained Nuclear Chain Reaction"), the charismatic American physicist J. Robert Oppenheimer, in 1943, directed the establishment of a laboratory in what was then a remote mesa at Los Alamos, New Mexico. Here, some of the most prominent of the world's scientists gathered to complete the transformation of theoretical physics into a working bomb.

The raw materials were two radioactive isotopes, uranium 235 and plutonium 239, which were supremely difficult to obtain and which were required in sufficient quantity to create critical mass. Under U.S. Army general Leslie R. Groves, giant secret plants at Oak Ridge, Tennessee, and at Hanford, Washington, were constructed to separate uranium 235 from its natural companion isotope, uranium 238 (this was done at Oak Ridge), and to produce plutonium 239 (at Hanford). At Los Alamos, the scientists had to devise a way to reduce these fissionable products to pure metal, which could be shaped in order to bring the chain reaction to an explosive level. The material also had to be brought together instantly to achieve a supercritical mass, which would create an explosion. Moreover, the scientists had to figure out how to make all of this compact enough to be carried to a target by an airplane.

By the summer of 1945, sufficient amounts of plutonium 239 were available from the Hanford Works, and the physicists at Los

Alamos had designed a bomb, a device using conventional high explosives to compress the shaped plutonium tightly and instantaneously together, so that it would go supercritical and create a massively energetic chain reaction: an atomic detonation.

The first test of the bomb, code named "Trinity," took place in the Alamogordo desert near Los Alamos at 0529:45 on July 16, 1945. All who witnessed it described it in much the same terms: the explosion of a sun on earth.

The next month, on August 6, 1945, at 8:15 A.M. local time, a single B-29 Superfortress bomber, christened *Enola Gay* by pilot Paul Tibbets in honor of his mother, dropped a uranium-235 bomb on Hiroshima, Japan. The device bore the innocuous nickname of "Little Man," and it destroyed two-thirds of the city, killing tens of thousands instantly and more who succumbed to radiation sickness later. (By the end of 1945, 140,000 were dead.) Another bomb, a plutonium-239 device called "Fat Man," was dropped on Nagasaki on August 9. Of 270,000 people present at the time of the detonation, about 70,000 would be dead by the end of the year. Japan, for the first time in its entire history, surrendered to a foreign power, and the "Atomic Age" exploded into the reality of the modern world.

1945

Salvador Edward Luria and Alfred Day Hershey Discover Viral Mutation

Independently of one another, the American microbiologists Salvador Edward Luria and Alfred Day Hershey demonstrated that viruses are subject to mutation, just as plants and animals are. This insight explained the difficulty of acquiring immunity to certain viral diseases. One might develop antibodies for one strain of a given virus, but the antibodies might not be effective against a mutated strain. A key (and highly vexing) disease process had been discovered.

1946

John William Mauchly and John P. Eckert, Jr., Design ENIAC, the First Fully Electronic Computer

The idea of a machine to perform calculations goes back at least as far as the abacus, which the Egyptians were using by 500 B.C. (see sidebar: "The Abacus, About 500 B.C."). It was not until 1822 that Charles Babbage and Lady Ada Lovelace began to develop the first computer in the modern sense: an "analytical engine" (as they called it), which was distinguished from a mere calculating device by the fact that it could be *programmed* to perform *any* logical operation capable of being expressed symbolically (see "1822: Charles Babbage and Lady Ada Lovelace Begin to Develop the First Modern Computer"). The pair never completed the machine.

It was the 1880 U.S. census that provided the next major impetus for the development of the computer. Following that event, worried officials estimated that the upcoming 1890 census would not be counted until 1902—two years *after* the 1900 census. Worse, the lag would become greater with each succeeding census. John Shaw Billings, a U.S. Army surgeon in charge of vital statistics at the Census Bureau, had the idea of using punch-hole cards to record and then process census information, and he gave the project to Herman Hollerith, who developed the cards and an electric machine to read them. Using the Hollerith machine, the 1890 census was completed in less than three years. Hollerith subsequently joined CTR (the

Computing Tabulating Recording Company), which later became International Business Machines—IBM.

By 1935, programmed electromechanical calculating devices were common in business. The next year, an English mathematician named Alan Turing formulated the essentials of modern computer science by developing the "Turing machine" (see "1936: Alan Turing Creates Computer Science with the Turing Machine").

With the outbreak of World War II, Turing joined the British team of mathematicians and others working to break the German "Enigma" code. In the meantime, across the Atlantic, IBM joined with a development team at Harvard University in 1939 to begin work on the Mark I, an advanced electromechanical device completed in 1944 and generally acknowledged to be the first truly modern programmable computer.

Yet it was only a prelude to what two University of Pennsylvania engineering professors, John William Mauchly and John P. Eckert, Jr., unveiled in 1946. "ENIAC" (Electronic Numerical Integrator and Computer) replaced the slow and cumbersome mechanical relays of Mark I and earlier devices with electronic "switches"—that is, vacuum tubes, eighteen *thousand* vacuum tubes—enabling it to perform very complex mathematical tasks with what was then unheard of speed and accuracy. The electronic behemoth, 3,000 cubic feet in volume, took up an entire room and weighed in at thirty tons. It kept a small army of technicians hopping to replace vacuum tubes, which burned out with great frequency. Although ENIAC was fully programmable, that task required extensive rewiring of massive switchboards and was, therefore, a major undertaking.

Realizing that ENIAC was unwieldy, Mauchly and Eckert acted on the suggestions of the mathematician John von Neumann and the American scientist John V. Atanasoff to develop UNIVAC (Universal Automatic Computer) in 1951. This differed from ENIAC in two very important respects. Programming was recorded on magnetic tape rather than accomplished by rewiring a switchboard, and UNIVAC was meant to be mass produced. There were still, of course, many difficulties to be overcome. Like ENIAC, UNIVAC was massive and depended on inherently unreliable vacuum tubes. But the work of Mauchly and Eckert had nevertheless changed our lives and created an industry. Over the next forty years, as electronic technology rapidly developed and the vacuum tube gave way to the transistor and the transistor to the integrated circuit ("chip"), computers would become progressively smaller, less expensive, more powerful, and, finally, ubiquitous, finding their way from government and military agencies, academia, business, and industry, into the home.

Charles Yeager, an American Test Pilot, Breaks the Sound Barrier in a Bell X-1

The speed of sound is generally placed at 1,088 feet per second at sea level at 32°F—about 740 miles per hour. The development of jet aircraft (see "1941: Using an Engine Design Patented in 1930 by Frank Whittle, the First Jet Plane Is Flown") greatly increased the maximum velocity of airplanes, and flying at the speed of sound came to seem an attainable goal.

Engineers spoke of this as the "sound barrier," because it did pose an aerodynamic challenge. At speeds under 740 miles per hour, air molecules slip smoothly over the surfaces of the plane, but, as the aircraft approaches the speed of sound, those molecules cannot move out of the way before they are overtaken. In effect, the air molecules pile up in front of the aircraft, forcing it to fly into a "wall" of compressed air. Some aeronautical engineers feared that hitting this wall would cause an aircraft to disintegrate. The engineers of the Bell Aircraft Company created an ultrastreamlined design, the X-1, which they hoped would minimize the effects of compressed-air turbulence.

On October 14, 1947, U.S. Air Force test pilot Charles E. Yeager flew the Bell X-1 faster than the speed of sound. Observers on the ground heard a loud "sonic boom," the effect of air piling up, suddenly slipping to one side of the aircraft, then rapidly reexpanding with a boom, like the crack of a giant whip.

1947

Dennis Gabor Lays the Theoretical Groundwork for the Development of Holography

P hotography is a two-dimensional medium because it records, chemically, the effect of a reflected-light image on a two-dimensional plane—photographic film. The Hungarian-born British physicist Dennis Gabor theorized, in 1947, that photography could be made three-dimensional. He proposed that a beam of light be split, so that part of it illuminated the object to be photographed, reflecting the surface of that object, no matter how irregular, and the other part of the light would be reflected from a mirror, without creating any irregularities. The two beams would come together again at the photographic film, which would record the interference pattern created by their convergence. By passing light through the developed film, the interference pattern would appear, creating not a two-dimensional image, but a *holograph* (the "holo" prefix meaning whole or entire) in three dimensions.

When Gabor proposed holography in 1947, the technology did not yet exist to transform theory into reality. Within less than three decades, advances in optics and, especially, the invention of the laser (see "1960: Theodore Harold Maiman Builds the First Laser") would make holography physically feasible.

1947

Willard Frank Libby Pioneers Carbon-14 Dating

The radioactive isotope carbon 14 was discovered in 1940 by Martin David Kamen. As with all radioactive isotopes, the radioactivity of carbon 14 degrades with time; however, as Kamen noted, this isotope has a very long half-life (the time it takes for the substance to decay to 50 percent of its radioactivity): 5,700 years.

Seven years after the discovery of carbon 14, the American chemist Willard Frank Libby took note of this long half-life and also of the fact that, due to cosmic ray bombardment of the earth, some of the nitrogen 14 in the atmosphere is converted into carbon 14. Thus new carbon 14 is always being formed as the old carbon 14 breaks down, creating a balance between old and new carbon 14. It occurred to Libby that plants absorb carbon dioxide during photosynthesis, so that carbon atoms, including trace amounts of carbon 14, would be present in plant tissue. Once the plant died, it would absorb no more carbon or carbon 14; therefore, the carbon 14 within the plant tissue would break down without being replaced. That is, only old carbon 14 would be present in the tissue. Using instruments to detect beta radiation, Libby concluded, it would be possible to measure the concentration of carbon 14 and, based on its half-life, determine how long ago the plant had died. Plants, of course, are used in many artifacts, including wooden objects, parchment, cloth, and so on. Therefore, carbon-14 dating techniques could be applied to human-made products, such as objects found in tombs or at archaeological sites. Science now had a tool to date the most ancient of archaeological finds, even in the absence of historical documentation.

1948

George Gamow Formulates the "Big Bang" Theory of the Origin of the Universe

Born Georgi Antonovich Gamow in Odessa, Russia, George Gamow emigrated to the United States in 1934, anglicized his name, and became professor of physics at George Washington University in Washington, D.C. His special interest was cosmology, the origin, nature, and fate of the universe. Gamow was especially interested in three theories, those of the Dutch astronomer Willem de Sitter, the Russian mathematician Alexander Alexandrovich Friedmann, and the Belgian astrophysicist Georges Henri Lemaître.

In 1917, de Sitter, pursuing the implications of Albert Einstein's general theory of relativity (see "1916: Einstein Advances the General Theory of Relativity, Thereby Establishing the Science of Cosmology"), concluded that the universe is not static, but is expanding (see "1917: Using Einstein's Relativity Equations, Astronomer Willem de Sitter Calculates That the Universe Is Expanding"). In 1922, Friedmann—one of Gamow's teachers—created equations that took the mass of the universe into account and seemed to confirm de Sitter's concept of an expanding universe. Then, in 1927, Lemaître pondered the implications of an expanding universe, concluding that if the universe expands as time goes forward, it would contract if time were imagined to run in reverse. Lemaître reasoned that the implication of an *expanding* universe is that it began from what must have been a small, highly compressed body, which Lemaître called the "cosmic egg." How did it begin to expand? Lemaître believed that it must have exploded, sending out of itself the matter that is now the universe. The expansion of the universe is the ongoing thrust of the original explosion.

Gamow synthesized all three theories into a fully developed cosmology. He showed how the chemical elements were formed in the aftermath of the explosion, and he theorized that the blast had been unimaginably energetic, but that the universe had necessarily cooled as it expanded, so that it was now, on average, only a few degrees above absolute zero ($217.15°K$). Gamow believed that such a temperature would create a background of microwave radiation emanating at a certain wavelength. At the time, the technology did not exist to measure such radiation, but radio astronomers did detect it in 1964—compelling empirical evidence of Gamow's theory.

In 1948, many were impressed by Gamow's hypothesis. Not so, however, the eminent British astronomer Sir Fred Hoyle, who derided it as a "big bang." Unintentionally, that good-naturedly mocking phrase stuck, and it even served to popularize what most astronomers now believe is the most plausible theory of the origin of the universe.

1948

William Shockley, Walter Brattain, and John Bardeen Invent the Transistor

In 1906, the American physicist Lee De Forest exploited a phenomenon known as the "Edison Effect" to create the Audion vacuum tube, a device that amplified a weak current, such as that produced by radio-frequency signals. In countless variations, the vacuum tube became the basis of all electronic circuits, from radio and television to the first electronic computers (see "1946: John William Mauchly and John P. Eckert, Jr., Design ENIAC, the First Fully Electronic Computer").

The vacuum tube is, in effect, an electronic valve, a necessary control for doing much of anything useful with electronics. Admirable though it was, the tube was plagued by many shortcomings. It was delicate, it burned out readily, it often operated unreliably or erratically, and it required relatively high voltages to operate.

The "Edison Effect," 1883

In 1883, while working on improvements to his incandescent electric light, Edison decided to see if putting a metal wire into the bulb, near, but not contacting, the filament, might improve the vacuum in the sealed bulb and thereby extend the useful life of the filament.

As it turned out, the wire did no such thing, but it did produce another phenomenon: a flow of current from the filament to the wire, across the gap separating them. Edison himself could think of no useful application for what was immediately dubbed the "Edison Effect," but, as applied in 1906 by Lee De Forest, it would prove to be a cornerstone of electronic technology.

Electrical engineers began looking for something to replace the vacuum tube, and, in 1948, Walter Houser Brattain, John Bardeen, and William Bradford Shockley, all scientists working for Bell Laboratories, collaborated on the semiconductor, a device that can control the electrical current that flows between two terminals by means of a low voltage applied to a third terminal. In short, it was an alternative electronic valve.

The three inventors called the most basic semiconductor device the transistor, which was a crystal grown from germanium, an element with excellent semiconductor properties. Later, silicon, much more abundant and cheaper than germanium, was found to possess equally suitable semiconductor properties. With this, the transistor emerged as a less expensive, more reliable, more efficient, lighter, and more compact alternative to the vacuum tube.

The transistor enabled the creation of ever more complex and affordable electronic devices, starting in the 1950s with portable "transistor radios," but soon finding uses in a dazzling array of sophisticated applications. By the 1960s, the individual transistor was being miniaturized to microscopic dimensions and incorporated into thin wafers of silicon called integrated circuits (ICs), chips, or microchips. The trend toward miniaturization and then microminiaturization created a virtually unlimited horizon for electronic technology (see "1960: Integrated Circuits—Chips—Are Introduced").

1948

Auguste Piccard Invents the Bathyscaphe

I n 1934, the American scientist Charles William Beebe created the bathysphere, a spherical diving bell with a heavy quartz window designed for very deep descents into the ocean. Using this craft, Beebe reached a record depth of 3,028 feet. Extraordinary as this achievement was, Beebe's bathysphere, tethered to a surface vessel, could not explore freely and independently. The daring French high-altitude balloonist Auguste Piccard decided to turn his attention from the upper atmosphere to the depths of the ocean and designed what he called a *bathyscaphe* ("ship of the deep"), which was an untethered very-deep-water one-man submarine. The first descent reached 4,500 feet, and, subsequently, the vessel was used to explore ocean depths few human beings had imagined and none had ever seen. The oceans, by far the largest features of earth, accounting for seven-tenths of the planet's surface, were at last opened to detailed scientific exploration.

Harold Urey and Stanley Miller
Model the Origin of Life

The American chemists Stanley Miller and Harold Urey conducted a remarkable experiment in an attempt to model the chemical and atmospheric conditions that produced life on earth, presumably more than four billion years ago. Within the confines of a five-liter flask, they created what they surmised to have been earth's primordial atmosphere, consisting of methane, hydrogen, ammonia, and water. They then wired the flask for an electric discharge, a spark they intended to simulate a source of ultraviolet photons. On the primordial earth, this source might have been lightning or some other form of energy, such as the shock wave of a meteor impact.

The result of the Miller-Urey experiment was not life, but it did create the organic constituents of life: amino acids, sugars, nucleotide bases, and other organic compounds. At the very least, the Miller-Urey experiment showed that, in the presence of certain chemicals and with the application of energy, the chemical building blocks of life would be created. In subsequent years, other scientists repeated and refined the Miller-Urey experiment, producing an even wider variety of organic molecules. The implications were unmistakable: The origin of life is consistent with the known laws of chemistry and physics and, apparently, required no supernatural intervention.

1952

Robert Wallace Wilkins Identifies the Tranquilizing Properties of Reserpine

During the first half of the twentieth century and earlier, institutions for the mentally ill were terrifying places. Some patients lived in dread of horrors only they knew. Others were uncontrollably violent, a danger to others and to themselves. For the first group, little could be done. For the second, there was no choice but a life of confinement, often under very harsh conditions.

As a last resort, barbiturate drugs could be administered. These, however, brought patients to a drowsy, subalert state. Barbiturates controlled behavior, but only by inducing a kind of suspended animation.

An alternative to incarceration and heavy drugging was identified in 1952 by the American physician Robert Wallace Wilkins, who reported his research on reserpine, a drug obtained from the root of a native American plant. Reserpine could produce sedation without diminishing alertness or bringing about sleep. Reserpine became the first in a galaxy of tranquilizers, a new class of drugs that transformed the treatment of the mentally ill and eased the lot of the chronically anxious.

Francis Crick and James Watson Postulate the Double-Helix Structure of DNA

In 1944, Oswald Avery identified DNA as the bearer of genetic information in living organisms (see "1944: Oswald Avery Discovers the Genetic Significance of DNA"), and in 1952, the British biophysicist Rosalind Elsie Franklin used an X-ray diffraction technique to explore the structure of the DNA molecule, discovering that it was a helix. Using one of Franklin's X-ray diffraction photographs, the American biochemist James Watson and the British physicist Francis Crick took the analysis of the structure of the DNA much further by explaining that it was two chains of nucleotides arranged as a *double* helix, resembling a spirally twisted ladder. The twisting sides of this ladder, Watson and Crick determined, consisted of alternate phosphate-sugar groups, while the rungs of the ladder were protein bases joined by weak hydrogen bonds. This double-helix structure enables DNA to replicate itself, which it does prior to cellular reproduction. When a cell divides to form two new cells, the double-stranded helix unwinds, the two sides of the ladder, in effect, unzipping, and each unzipped strand picks up complementary nucleotides, which, incorporated into those unzipped strands, create two new DNA molecules that are identical to each other and to the original molecule. Because the DNA molecule carries chemically coded genetic information for the transmission of inherited traits, when the double helix "unzips," that coded information is passed on.

As Watson and Crick explained, DNA has a dual function. The

process of replication of DNA during reproduction ensures that a baby born to a human mother and a human father will be a human being and not a mouse, a baboon, or a kumquat. Moreover, the DNA ensures that the offspring will inherit certain more specific genetic traits from the mother and father. However, even as DNA transmits characteristics common to the species and to the parents, it also ensures that each individual is unique.

In the case of human beings, each cell has twenty-three pairs of chromosomes containing the full DNA code, which is nothing less than the blueprint for everything needed to build the individual. One member of each chromosomal pair is inherited from the mother, and one from the father. The unique DNA pattern that results from this is copied in each and every cell of the body.

Maurice Ewing and Bruce Heezen Develop Plate Tectonics, the Study of the Evolution of the Earth's Crust

Maurice Ewing and Bruce Heezen, American *physicists,* made a *geological* discovery: a canyon or rift that runs along the Mid-Oceanic Ridge, a great, world-surrounding undersea mountain range. The scientists concluded that the rift actually broke the earth's crust into gigantic but distinctly defined plates, butted together as if by a carpenter. From this latter quality, Ewing and Heezen called the plates *tectonic plates,* from the Greek word for carpenter.

The discovery of the tectonic plates took geology to a new macro level, encompassing the entire earth as a single geologic system. Of the six major plates (there are also additional minor ones), the one that includes most of the Pacific Ocean was found to account for more than three-quarters of the energy released as earthquakes on the planet. The movement of the plates, relative to one another, explains much about seismic activity and has led to unprecedented understanding of earthquake phenomena.

1954

Jonas Salk Develops a Successful Polio Vaccine

Poliomyelitis—infantile paralysis, or polio—had long been a dread disease, but beginning in 1942, it assumed truly terrifying epidemic proportions in the United States (and elsewhere) each summer. Cruelest of all, "infantile paralysis" usually struck infants and young children. For some, it came and went, having created no symptoms worse than a transitory case of the flu. For some, it was fatal. And for others—about 20 percent of those infected—polio resulted in paralysis. This varied greatly in severity. In some cases, the paralysis was temporary. In others, permanent, ranging from partial paralysis, to paraplegia, to paralysis so devastating that the nerves controlling respiration were damaged, so that the victim could breathe only with the aid of an "iron lung," a massive respirator that resembled nothing more than the iron maiden of medieval torture. In the worst epidemic year, 1950, there were 33,344 cases of polio in the United States, and summer became a season of anxiety, with public swimming pools closed and parents agonizing whenever they let their children play with others.

A young American physician, Jonas Salk, completed his training at New York University's medical school and, rather than go into practice, took up research on immunology under Dr. Thomas Francis at the University of Michigan. This institution produced the world's first killed-virus vaccine against influenza—a major breakthrough, because while scientists believed that vaccines prepared from dead bacteria were effective in immunizing against bacterial infections, they were persuaded that immunization against viruses required live-virus vaccines. And that was a dangerous proposition. Inoculating a patient with live viruses might very well result in infection with the very disease one was trying to prevent.

Moving to the University of Pittsburgh, Salk worked on a killed-virus vaccine for polio, and by 1954 had produced enough to begin patient testing. The following year, the U.S. Food and Drug Administration pronounced the "Salk vaccine" both safe and effective, and a nationwide vaccination campaign got under way. Within a very short time, polio was conquered.

George C. Devol, Jr., and Joseph Engelberger Patent a Robot

The notion of an automaton—a "mechanical man"—is quite old; during the eighteenth century, for instance, various charlatans claimed to have invented chess-playing automatons (which, invariably, proved to be humans disguised as mechanical men). Then in 1920, the Czech playwright Karel Čapek presented *R.U.R.*, which stood for Rossum's Universal Robots and was a political drama that centered on mechanical men manufactured as workers or serfs—the word "robot" is derived from a Czech word that can apply to either. The play is now largely forgotten outside of the Czech Republic, but the word *robot* stuck, and it served to revive the age-old interest in artificial beings, especially those that could perform useful—perhaps even superhuman—work.

The first actual patent on a robotic device was secured by the American inventor George C. Devol, Jr., financed by the visionary entrepreneur Joseph Engelberger. Over a period of two decades, the pair created robots to perform a variety of manufacturing tasks. These early devices were limited by the relatively rudimentary level of computer science at the time, but they were the start of an increasingly important robotics industry.

Surgeons in Boston Perform the First Successful Organ Transplant, a Kidney

Surgeons had long recognized that, in the event of the failure of an organ, death might be prevented by transplanting a healthy organ from another person. In the case of organs that are doubled in the body—the kidney—or that at least partially regenerate—the liver—the donation can come from a living volunteer. In the case of other organs, they can be "harvested" from persons very recently killed, typically by such sudden trauma as an automobile accident.

But it soon became apparent that, in most cases, the recipient's body rejects the donated organ, reacting to it as a foreign infection or as an allergen. In 1954, Boston surgeons determined that the only sure way around rejection was to make a transplant only from one identical twin to another—since identical twins are genetic duplicates. The first successful organ transplant, that of a kidney, was performed, and the recipient lived for eight years.

Since that time, transplant researchers have continued to develop tests for compatibility between recipients and donors who are not identical twins, and to find drugs and other treatments to suppress the immune reaction in the recipient, thereby suppressing organ rejection. Success has varied, but organ transplantation is now a common procedure.

The Soviet Union Launches *Sputnik,* the First Artificial Satellite

Robert Goddard, an American, developed the principles of liquid-fuel rocketry beginning in 1926 (see "1926: Robert Goddard Fires the First Liquid-Fuel Rocket"), but it was the Germans, during World War II, who made the most significant strides by developing the rocket as a weapon of terror. At the end of that war, both the United States and the Soviet Union began rocket-development programs by studying captured German V-1 and V-2 rockets and by employing the services of the German scientists who had developed them. For both countries, these scientists made up the core of national space programs, and although the most prominent of the German rocket scientists, Wernher von Braun, came to the United States, it was the Soviet Union that successfully orbited the first artificial satellite.

It was launched on October 4, 1957, from a site deep within the interior of the country. *Sputnik*—Russian for "traveler" or "satellite"—was no more impressive than its mundane name: a thirty-eight-pound metal sphere that contained only a radio transmitter and sported antennas. Yet it was nothing less than a new moon.

The sole purpose of *Sputnik* was to orbit the earth and broadcast radio beeps to enable tracking. However, to the Soviets, the satellite seemed a vindication of communism over democracy, and to the United States, it was a wake-up call. As many Americans saw it, *Sputnik* portended military disaster—the Soviet occupation of outer space, the ultimate high ground, from which weapons might be wielded against the United States. For others, it was simply a stinging attack on American pride.

In either case, the successful orbiting of *Sputnik* was the starting gun in a "space race" between the USSR and the United States.

First Communications Satellite, 1965

The first satellite with a practical, commercial use was developed by scientists in the United States. *Early Bird,* launched on April 6, 1965, was the world's first communications satellite. Two hundred forty voice communication circuits and one channel for television were available. This was the start of an orbiting network of satellites, which, well before the century was out, would transform the nature of communications on every level.

1959

The Soviet Union Launches the First Moon Probe

I n the space race triggered by the triumph of *Sputnik* (see "1957: The Soviet Union Launches *Sputnik,* the First Artificial Satellite"), the United States got off to a slow, stumbling start. The first several American launches after *Sputnik* were abject failures, and it wasn't until January 1958 that *Explorer I* was successfully orbited. However, on January 2, 1959, the Soviets stunned the world yet again by launching *Lunik I.* It was the first rocket to achieve and surpass escape velocity—about seven miles per second—the speed necessary to break free of the gravitational field of the earth.

That was a triumph in itself—although *Lunik I* failed in its stated mission, to land on the moon. It missed and ended up orbiting the sun, thereby becoming the first artificial planet. Later in the year, on September 12, *Lunik II* was launched, and it succeeded in hitting the moon—thereby becoming the first human-made object to reach another world. Less than a month after this, on October 4, *Lunik III* swung round the far side of the moon, sending back the first-ever images of something never before seen: the hemisphere of the moon perpetually hidden from earth.

Integrated Circuits—Chips—Are Introduced

E lectronic circuits require the equivalent of valves to control current flow in myriad useful ways. The first valves were vacuum tubes, which were almost completely replaced by transistors (see "1948: William Shockley, Walter Brattain, and John Bardeen Invent the Transistor"). Among other things, the development of the transistor was the first major step toward the miniaturization of electronics—an evolutionary trend that continued apace during the 1950s. In 1960, each individual transistor could be made so small that it was no longer necessary to treat them as individual components. It now became both practical and desirable to manufacture transistors as components integrated into complete electronic circuits and subassemblies: *integrated circuits.*

ICs are small, thin wafers of silicon (or other semiconductor material), which are microscopically etched with transistor circuits. Because the wafers, originally about a quarter-inch square, resembled nondescript chips, they were informally and universally called chips.

Just about any electronic circuit can be designed onto a chip, and the chips can then be assembled into a wide variety of devices. Over a remarkably short period of time, the degree of specialization and complexity of available chips grew exponentially, so that now the chip at the heart of a desktop computer—the "microprocessor"—is, in effect, the computer itself. All of the other devices boxed along with the chip—hard drive, sound card, video card, and so on—are entirely subordinate to this small semiconductor wafer. The integrated circuit brought electronics into virtually every space and aspect of modern civilized life.

1960

Theodore Harold Maiman
Builds the First Laser

In 1953, the American physicist Charles Hard Townes created the Maser (microwave amplification by stimulated emission of radiation), a device that bombarded with photons the molecules of ammonia vapor to create a high-intensity microwave beam. The maser principle was based on Albert Einstein's observation that if a photon of a certain size strikes a molecule, that molecule will absorb the photon and be elevated to a higher energy level. If, however, the molecule that was struck was already at a higher energy level, it will return to the lower energy level and, in the process, emit a photon of the same wavelength and moving in the same direction as the striking photon. Thus, two photons are set into motion, which then strike two more high-energy-level molecules, thereby producing four photons. Multiplied many times over, this process creates a flood of photons, all of identical wavelength and all moving in exactly the same direction (they constitute "coherent radiation"). In practical terms, the photon beam that results is extremely intense.

The maser principle was first applied to *visible* light by the American physicist Theodore Harold Maiman in 1960. He used a ruby rod through which an intense flash lamp emitted light that was thereby concentrated in a coherent beam into a tiny point that created temperatures hotter than the sun's surface. At first dubbed an optical maser, the device soon got a name of its own: *laser*, for light amplification by stimulated emission of radiation.

Initially, the intense laser beam was seen as a cutting tool or even a weapon, but it is now even more extensively used as a device for transmitting, recording, and reading digital data, music, and video.

1961

The Soviet Union Sends
Yury Gagarin into Space

Shortly after the successful orbital mission of *Sputnik* (see "1957: The Soviet Union Launches *Sputnik*, the First Artificial Satellite"), the Soviets lofted a dog into orbit, then, in 1960, launched two missions with dogs—and brought both of them back alive. Clearly, like the United States, the Soviets were preparing for manned space flight, and, on April 12, 1961, they launched "cosmonaut" Yury Gagarin into space, sending him on a single orbit around the earth. The United States sent its first "astronaut," Alan B. Shepard, into space a month later—but only on a fifteen-minute suborbital flight. It would be nine months before John Glenn embarked on an American orbital mission, by which time the Soviets had orbited a second cosmonaut—Gherman Stepanovich Titov—*seventeen* times around the earth in a daylong mission on August 6, 1961.

1961

Murray Gell-Mann Describes Quarks

Particle physics, the science of subatomic particles, was exploding by the mid-twentieth century. To the well-understood atomic particles—protons, electrons, and neutrons—were added a host of "intermediate" subatomic particles, including the muon (or lepton, described in 1937), the pi-meson (or pion, described in 1947), and the so-called strange particles, the kaons and hyperons.

The discovery of so many particles was exciting but also overwhelming and puzzling, especially since they seemed to act in contradictory ways. The American physicist Murray Gell-Mann, who had already researched "strange particles," developed a means of grouping subatomic particles into families, which he called the Eightfold Way. The most exciting aspect of his classification system was that, as with the periodic table of the elements (see "1869: Dmitry Ivanovich Mendeleyev Creates the Periodic Table of the Elements"), it contained gaps, which Gell-Mann believed indicated the existence of particles yet to be discovered.

Gell-Mann's particle families were based on what he called *quarks* (the word was borrowed from James Joyce's arcane novel *Finnigans Wake*). These were a small set of particles, Gell-Mann theorized, each complemented by an antiquark, which, grouped together in varying combinations, accounted for all of the particles known as hadrons (including proton, neutron, lambda, sigma, xi, pion, kaon, J particle, and omega). That is, the hadrons were said to be composed of quarks.

The most revolutionary aspect of Gell-Mann's quark was that it carried fractional charges—for instance, plus or minus one-third or two-thirds. This goes against all that is known about the nature of electrical charges, yet it was undeniable that the quark accounted for so much in particle physics that even the notion of fractional charges won acceptance. As for Gell-Mann, the importance of his work in opening up the subatomic world was recognized by a Nobel Prize in 1969.

Various Astronomers Identify
a New Kind of Heavenly Body,
the Quasar (Quasistellar Radio Source)

One of the cosmic mysteries radioastronomy revealed was a set of very strong sources of radio signals emanating from objects that appeared to be very dim stars. How could such faint objects be responsible for such powerful signals? Indeed, because the disparity between the dimness of the objects and the strength of the radio signals was so striking, it was by no means certain that these objects were, in fact, stars, so they were dubbed quasistellar radio sources, or *quasars*.

And there was more strangeness to come. Spectrographic studies of the quasars revealed lines that could not be identified, that corresponded to no known elements. In 1963, the Dutch-born American astronomer Maarten Schmidt observed that the lines did make sense if they were viewed as the lines that would normally be in the ultraviolet portion of the spectrum, but had been displaced by a great redshift. The redshift phenomenon was first described in 1848 by the French physicist Armand-Hippolyte-Louis Fizeau, who pointed out that the Doppler effect (see "1842: Christian Johann Doppler Describes the Doppler Effect, a Cornerstone of Modern Astronomy"), which applied to sound waves, also applied to light waves. That is, just as the wavelength of a sound wave became longer as the source of the sound receded from the listener, so the wavelength of light waves would become greater if the source of the light receded from the observer. This effect would be apparent in a shift in the dark lines of the spectra. If the light source was approaching, the lines would shift toward the ultraviolet (shorter wavelength). If it was receding, the lines would shift toward the infrared (longer wavelength). This latter phenomenon astronomers subsequently called a redshift.

The detection of an enormous redshift in the quasar spectra signified that these sources were extremely distant, well over a billion light-years away. Dim though they were, the fact that they were detectable at all at such a distance meant that quasars had to be extremely energetic. Thus it was concluded that quasars are not stars, but galaxies with highly active centers. Moreover, some are at least 12 billion light-years away.

Now, that fact alone is astounding. But if we take into account the Big Bang theory (see "1948: George Gamow Formulates the 'Big Bang' Theory of the Origin of the Universe") as well as Willem de Sitter's idea of an expanding universe (see "1917: Using Einstein's Relativity Equations, Astronomer Willem de Sitter Calculates That the Universe Is Expanding"), then it becomes apparent that quasars are not merely very distant objects, but very old ones, objects that have expanded with the universe over billions of years and that appear to us now as messengers from a time very near to that of the Big Bang itself.

1965

Elso Sterrenberg Barghoorn Discovers Microfossils, Windows on the Precambrian World

Fossils had been studied for years, but none older than about 600 million years—from the era of the dawn of the Cambrian era—had ever been found. The reason was simple. Organisms of the Precambrian era lacked shells and hard tissue; therefore, they rarely fossilized, but simply died without leaving a trace.

In 1965, the American paleontologist Elso Sterrenberg Barghoorn sought to push the fossil record as far back as possible by studying microscopic bits of carbonized material from very old rocks. His intuition was that these would reveal fossilized evidence of the bacteria that had been among the very first forms of life on earth. He made use of the electron microscope (see "1932: Ernst August Friedrich Ruska Builds the First Electron Microscope"), which revealed microfossils within the material, presumably dating back some 3.5 billion years. The microfossil record suggests that the earth was no more than a billion years old before the first forms of life began to appear on it.

MODERN
SCIENCE

1967

Robert Briggs, Thomas J. King, and John B. Gurdon Develop Cloning Techniques

Cloning is not unknown in nature. The very word *clone* is Greek for twig and reflects the fact that a twig may be grafted onto the branch of another tree and then grow. A variety of simple animal organisms—flatworms are a familiar example, as are starfish—can regenerate from a tiny portion of tissue.

Among the more complex animals, cloning does not occur naturally; however, in 1967, the British biologist John B. Gurdon employed the technique of nuclear transplantation (developed by the American biologists Robert Briggs and Thomas J. King) to produce the first clone of a vertebrate animal. Gurdon took a cell from the intestine of a South African clawed frog and implanted it in the ovum (egg cell) of another frog, having first removed the nucleus from the ovum. From the ovum, with the transplanted nucleus, a new South African clawed frog developed and was hatched.

At this point, cloning the more advanced vertebrates was years off. It was one thing to perform nuclear transplantation on an exposed amphibian egg, and quite another to carry out a cloning procedure on, say, a mammal, in which the ovum remains within the body (see "1996: Keith Campbell, Ian Wilmut, and Others of the Roslin Institute, U.K., Clone a Sheep from the Nucleus of a Specially Cultured Cell").

Astronomers Antony Hewish and Jocelyn Bell Are the First to Discover Pulsars

In the 1960s, the British astronomer Antony Hewish directed construction of a new radio observatory, an array of more than two thousand receivers deployed over three acres and intended to detect minute changes in microwave intensities. In 1967, one of Hewish's graduate students, Jocelyn Bell, detected a remarkable radio source from deep space. Located between the stars Vega and Altair, it emitted a signal burst for a fraction of a second, then fell silent for precisely 1.33730109 seconds. It did this with a precision far in excess of any human timepiece. Shortly after Bell's discovery, other astronomers identified such "pulsating stars," which were eventually dubbed *pulsars*.

In the 1970s, Hewish offered an explanation of the pulsar phenomenon. Because the signal bursts were so precise, he concluded that the source of radiation was both rotating and very compact. He reasoned that only a relatively small object would produce such crisp, clean bursts of energy; a star-sized object would emit a more diffuse signal. Hewish believed that the compact, spinning sources were neutron stars, the superdense compact cores of massive stars that had undergone a supernova explosion. Such neutron stars spin rapidly and, because they are so massive and so dense, they create a magnetic field many times stronger than that of the parent star, a magnetic field many trillions of times stronger than that of the earth. The combination of rapid rotation and a powerful magnetic field creates very strong radiation that is emitted at the star's magnetic poles. The radiation "shines" out of these poles much as light shines from a rotating lighthouse beacon. The beacon is visible only when it rotates toward an observer. The radiation burst of the pulsar is "visible" only when it rotates toward a radio telescope.

The discovery of pulsars, energetic neutron stars that are, except for black holes, the most densely massive objects in the universe, is wondrous in itself. Subsequently, however, some pulsars were discovered that exhibit minute variations in their pulsations. This astronomers attribute to the pulsar's wobbling on its axis. What causes wobbling? Gravity—or, more precisely, the gravitational influence of planets. Thus, some pulsars indicate the presence of extrasolar planets—worlds outside of our solar system (see "1995–1996: The Discovery of Extrasolar Planets Is Announced").

Neil Armstrong and Edwin "Buzz" Aldrin, American Astronauts, Land on the Moon

Since the Soviet launch of *Sputnik* in 1957 (see "1957: The Soviet Union Launches *Sputnik*, the First Artificial Satellite") and the Soviet orbiting of the first human being in space (see "1961: The Soviet Union Sends Yury Gagarin into Space"), the United States had been playing catch-up in the "space race." To many, indeed, the speech President John F. Kennedy made on May 25, 1961, rang hollow with what seemed an impossible objective: "I believe this nation should commit itself to achieving the goal, before the decade is out, of landing a man on the moon and returning him safely to earth. No single space project in this period will be more impressive to mankind, or more important for the long-range exploration of space, and none will be so difficult or expensive to accomplish." Nevertheless, the moon became the target of America's manned space program.

The program was called *Apollo,* and it was the biggest, most complex, and most daring scientific and technological venture in the history of humankind. A mighty *Saturn* V multistage booster would carry the three-man *Apollo* craft beyond earth orbit on a two-and-a-half-day voyage. *Apollo* would enter lunar orbit, then the lunar excursion module (LEM), called *Eagle,* with two men aboard, would separate from the orbiting command module to land on the moon. The astronauts would explore the lunar surface for a time, return to *Eagle,* lift off, and dock with the orbiting command module, which would then slingshot around the moon, blast out of lunar orbit, and return to earth.

Could anything of this magnitude actually be pulled off? The program did not begin well. *Apollo 1,* undergoing a launchpad test, was swept by a catastrophic fire on January 27, 1967, killing astronauts Virgil I. "Gus" Grissom, Edward H. White, and Roger B. Chaffee. At the very least, it seemed that the program would be greatly delayed; perhaps it would even be scrapped. But the National Aeronautics and Space Administration (NASA), Congress, and the American people had the will to carry on, and, after a series of preliminary missions, including earth- and moon-orbital flights, *Apollo 11* was launched on July 16, 1969, crewed by Neil A. Armstrong, Edwin E. "Buzz" Aldrin, Jr., and Michael Collins. It was Armstrong and Aldrin who piloted the *Eagle,* while Collins remained in orbit, flying the command module.

The landing came on July 20, at 4:17 Eastern Daylight Time (8:17 P.M. Greenwich Mean Time). With billions watching live television pictures beamed to radio telescope antennas on earth, Armstrong descended the *Eagle*'s ladder.

"That's one small step for [a] man," he declared as he jumped off the module's ladder, "one giant leap for mankind."

The two astronauts spent twenty-one hours thirty-six minutes on the moon, collecting lunar soil and "moon rocks" as well as setting up a number of experiments. The landing was the culmination of a human dream certainly older than history, and in a politically turbulent period racked by war, the lunar landing spoke of the human spirit and, however briefly, united humanity in one of its greatest achievements.

ARPANET, Precursor to the Internet, Is Activated

In 1999, Vice President Al Gore remarked in a CNN interview that "During my service in the United States Congress, I took the initiative in creating the Internet." To many, this sounded as if Gore were taking credit for having invented the Internet, and he was given a lot of media grief over the remark. But this begs the obvious question: Who *did* invent the Internet?

As usual with any complex technological system, no single person "invented" it. Indeed, the Internet is not so much an entity, a thing that was invented, as it is a state of being or a fact: the fact of the interconnectedness of millions of computers and computer networks. And once this vast network became well established by the beginning of the 1990s, it took on a life of its own as a space—or "cyberspace"—in which data, ideas, images, and thoughts are transmitted, exchanged, and shared, and in which an increasingly vast amount of commerce—buying, selling, and advertising—takes place. Combined with the personal computer (see "1981: IBM Introduces the Personal Computer"), the Internet connects many (potentially, all) businesses, institutions, government agencies, and households to each other and to the world.

Yet the Internet does have a physical and temporal origin. In 1969, the U.S. Department of Defense established ARPANET, the Advanced Research Projects Agency Network, a computer-mediated communications network intended to link U.S. military forces together and to connect them with a network of institutional and governmental computers. Very soon after ARPANET commenced operations, researchers, not only in defense, but in other academic fields, used it. As they used it, they also contributed to it, and the network expanded steadily.

At first, ARPANET and the subnetworks it engendered could be accessed only by large mainframe computers in universities, government establishments, and research-oriented industries. But as personal computers began to proliferate and as these were equipped with modems enabling them to receive and transmit data via the telephone lines, ARPANET blossomed into the Internet, ultimately exploding beyond the confines of any government, corporation, or institution. The American citizen—the American family—embarked on the "information superhighway."

1970

Hamilton Smith and Daniel Nathans Develop Recombinant DNA, First Step Toward Genetic Engineering

The genetic significance of DNA was well established by Crick and Watson in 1953 (see "1953: Francis Crick and James Watson Postulate the Double-Helix Structure of DNA"), and, in 1970, two American microbiologists, Hamilton Smith and Daniel Nathans, found an enzyme capable of cutting the DNA molecule at certain specific places. The DNA fragments that resulted still contained viable genetic information, which implied that fragments could be artificially recombined with other fragments to create new genes that did not exist in nature.

Smith and Nathans's discovery opened the door to the development of recombinant DNA, DNA that permits genetic engineering, the modification and transfer—or even wholesale design—of genes to create organisms with desired characteristics. The possibilities of genetic engineering with recombinant DNA are intensely exciting— the genetic prevention of cancer, for example—and also frightening— the engineering of someone's idea of a "super race."

Fiber Optics Are Introduced

Since the last third of the nineteenth century, people had been familiar with conducting electric current through silver or copper wire. By 1970, glass fibers had been created to do much the same with light. The fibers were manufactured such that they not only transmitted light, but their internal coating reflected light, which allowed the light to follow any path, no matter how curved. Combined with lasers (see "1960: Theodore Harold Maiman Builds the First Laser"), fiber optics meant that light could be used to carry enormous amounts of data, thereby greatly improving communications and other data-intensive technologies.

1972

CAT Scan Techniques Are Introduced

Wilhelm Röntgen's discovery of X rays in 1895 (see "1895: Wilhelm Conrad Röntgen Discovers X Rays") gave medical science a powerful diagnostic tool. Yet, because the X ray is essentially a photograph, it is a two-dimensional image of a three-dimensional space: the human body. To image the body in three dimensions, scientists developed computerized axial tomographic scanning, the CAT scan, which combines, by means of a computer, numerous X-ray images that, taken together, yield a three-dimensional cross-section of the body or area of the body under study. The CAT scan gives diagnosticians and surgeons a far more complete view and, in many instances, is a safe, noninvasive alternative to risky exploratory surgery.

1972

The Laser Disc Is Introduced

Sound was first recorded mechanically, on foil or wax cylinders (see "1877: Thomas Alva Edison Invents the Phonograph and Records Sound") and, later, on vinyl discs. The technology prevailed for more than a century—the only alternative being magnetic wire recording (introduced as early as 1898) or, later, magnetic tape (patented in Germany in 1928). Vinyl discs were bulky, fragile, and subject to inevitable wear. Tape was also vulnerable. Moreover, both technologies were severely limited in the amount of information they could record and reproduce.

In 1972, the laser (see "1960: Theodore Harold Maiman Builds the First Laser") was first used to produce sound recordings. An amplifier modulated a laser beam, which, in response, microscopically pitted a plastic-coated metal disc. In a playback device, another laser beam picked up the pits and translated them into a modulated beam, which was converted back into sound. The laser disc was soon made quite compact—in the form of a compact disc, or CD—and it was capable of recording a huge amount of information. This meant recording more music and theoretically with greater fidelity than a conventional long-playing phonograph record. Moreover, CDs did not wear out with repeated playing and were also far more stable than magnetic tape.

Within another dozen years, an improved version of the CD was developed, the digital versatile disc, or DVD, which was capable of carrying even more information, so that it could serve as a practical medium for recording high-fidelity video as well as audio. By the late 1990s, both the CD and DVD formats would find widespread application as media to record computer-readable data, a use hardly foreseen in the 1970s.

Edward P. Tryon Postulates That the Universe Is a "Random Quantum Fluctuation in a Vacuum," Meaning, in Effect, That It Originated from Nothing

Since the proposal of the Big Bang theory (see "1948: George Gamow Formulates the 'Big Bang' Theory of the Origin of the Universe"), cosmologists developed an extensive theoretical understanding of the probable evolution of the universe, including the first few fractions of a second after the initial "big bang." Yet accepting that the universe came into being as the result of an explosion of a supremely dense concentration of mass did not answer the most basic ontological question. Where did that mass, however infinitesimal, however dense, come from?

The American physicist Edward P. Tryon offered an explanation. A vacuum, a true vacuum—nothingness—can, according to quantum mechanics and the uncertainty principle, give rise to subatomic particles that disappear before they are detected. That is, within nothingness, particles will randomly appear and disappear. Randomly, from time to time, a particle may appear that is capable of developing the mass of the universe and that expands before it disappears. In this sense, then, the universe is a random quantum fluctuation in a vacuum, and thus did indeed originate from nothing.

F. Sherwood Rowland and Mario Molina Demonstrate That CFCs Have the Potential for Destroying the Earth's Ozone Layer

As human settlement of the planet has became increasingly industrial, pollution has become an increasingly serious problem, posing a significant threat to the quality and even the continuation of life on earth.

Some sources of pollution are obvious, for example, exhaust gases from combustion processes, especially those associated with industry and automobiles. Other sources are more subtle, but, potentially, even more catastrophic. In 1974, two American researchers, F. Sherwood Rowland and Mario Molina, demonstrated that chlorofluorocarbons (CFCs), the compounds contained in freon, tend to break down some components of the atmosphere, especially the ozone layer. Chlorofluorocarbons were introduced in the 1930s. Mistakenly thought to be inert, CFCs seemed the ideal industrial chemical—highly useful, relatively cheap, and apparently harmless—so that, by the 1970s, they had become ubiquitous as refrigerants and aerosol propellants. Cumulatively, large amounts of CFCs escaped into the atmosphere.

The ozone layer serves as a natural atmospheric shield that reduces the amount of ultraviolet radiation reaching the earth. An increase in ultraviolet radiation is associated with various cancers (especially skin cancers) and other diseases in human beings. Moreover, too much ultraviolet radiation may kill valuable soil bacteria and ocean plankton—a key element in the food chain—thereby greatly disrupting the planetary ecosystem.

Atmospheric observations subsequent to Rowland and Molina's research confirmed the thinning of ozone layer, especially above Antarctica, and the United States banned the use of CFC refrigerants and aerosol propellants in 1978.

1978

First "Test-Tube Baby" Is Born

People have always been fascinated by the idea of life produced, in some sense, artificially. The phrase "test-tube baby" is a media invention, smacking more of Frankenstein than of medical science, but it does have some validity as a description of what happened in England, on July 25, 1978.

On that day, a baby was born—not in a test tube, but from an ovum (egg) that had been fertilized outside of the womb, in laboratory glassware, using sperm donated by the father. The fertilized egg, after undergoing initial development, was then surgically reimplanted in the mother, where it continued to develop normally. The baby was also born normally.

The medical name for the "test-tube baby" process is *in vitro fertilization,* "vitro" being the Latin for glass. In vitro fertilization is used when, for various medical reasons, fertilization within the body (called *in vivo fertilization*) cannot take place.

1979

Walter Alvarez Finds a Reason for the Extinction of the Dinosaurs

Historians generally agree: The further back an event, the more difficult it is to find out anything concrete about it. One thing is for certain: The dinosaurs became extinct a very long time ago.

Scientists had long wondered why. Why had so varied and, apparently, so well adapted a species suddenly ceased to exist some 65 million years ago, the point at which the Mesozoic Era transitions into the Cenozoic?

The American scientist Walter Alvarez was studying sedimentation rates in certain rocks in Italy when he detected an abnormally large concentration of the rare metal iridium within a narrow layer of the rock he was investigating. This layer corresponded to the late Mesozoic and early Cenozoic era—the period that saw the extinction of the dinosaurs.

Alvarez concluded that the concentration of iridium and the death of the dinosaurs was no coincidence. But where would so much iridium come from? Alvarez speculated that a very large meteor—or even a comet—colliding with the earth could have been the source. Such an impact would have caused great natural catastrophes, including tidal waves, earthquakes, volcanic upheavals, and the like. Perhaps even more destructive would have been the great cloud of dust raised by the impact. It would have filtered out much of the sunlight for a very long time.

By no means was Alvarez's explanation of the extinction of the dinosaurs universally accepted in 1979 or even today; however, evidence of a catastrophic meteor impact (indeed, multiple significant impacts) continues to accumulate, and the Alvarez hypothesis has steadily gained credibility.

The United States Launches
the First Space Shuttle

The reality of both the Soviet and American space programs often rivaled science fiction's imaginings of space flight—except in one key respect. Science fiction writers almost invariably depicted space ships as vessels analogous to airplanes, which could be flown, landed, then flown again and again. Until 1981, all Soviet and American space flights had been made in one-way craft, space "capsules" lofted into orbit (or beyond) by nonreusable booster rockets, then returned to earth in a controlled descent. Soviet capsules parachuted onto the ground, whereas U.S. spacecraft parachuted to an oceanic "splashdown." In both cases, the capsules were not intended to be reused.

It is easier and faster to design "single-use" boosters and capsules than it is to engineer reusable spacecraft. This facilitated the kind of rapid development that a "space *race*" demanded. However, once the race had been won, American planners turned to the more demanding task of building of reusable vehicles, and the space shuttle was born. Although it was sent into orbit by a disposable booster rocket, the shuttle itself was capable of reentering the atmosphere and then, with its stubby delta wings, gliding to a non-powered landing on specially prepared fields.

The idea behind the space shuttle was to make space travel less expensive and more routine. Not only would the Shuttle be used to explore space, it would perform practical (and even profitable) tasks, such as placing satellites into orbit and flying personnel to and from orbiting space stations. The first space shuttle flight took place on April 12, 1981, and there have been many more since then. However, critics of manned space flight point out that the shuttle has never proven profitable, that the scientific information gathered from shuttle flights has been minimal, and that manned programs drain precious funding from more scientifically productive unmanned exploration. As two fatal accidents proved—the *Challenger* disaster on January 28, 1986, and the *Columbia* catastrophe on February 1, 2003—manned spaceflight is an inherently hazardous undertaking.

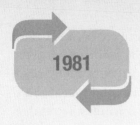

IBM Introduces the Personal Computer

Since 1946, when the first fully electronic computer was introduced (see "1946: John William Mauchly and John P. Eckert, Jr., Design ENIAC, the First Fully Electronic Computer"), computers assumed an increasingly important role in all aspects of life, from the most basic bookkeeping to the most advanced scientific research. Yet, to most people in the 1970s, computers were big, mysterious machines locked up in special rooms and so expensive that only mammoth corporations and the government could afford them. Then, in 1975, an article in the debut issue of *Popular Electronics* announced: "The era of the computer in every home—a favorite topic among science fiction writers—has arrived!"

The article was about the Altair 8800, a computer kit. Programmable not through software, but by means of an array of switches, the Altair 8800 produced its output not on a monitor screen, but by illuminating light-emitting diodes (LEDs) on its front panel. Today's desktop PC may contain 128 megabytes (128 million bytes) or, often, more of random-access memory (RAM); Altair maxed out at eight kilobytes (8,000 bytes). It was less a practical tool than an amusement for the geek hobbyist, and the *Popular Electronics* claim of a computer in every home was a bit premature.

But not by much. The Altair proved surprisingly popular, and by 1977, new companies such as Apple and Commodore were producing far more sophisticated computers running a relatively simple programming language (originally developed for large "main-frame" computers) called BASIC, which could be readily adapted to practical calculating and word-processing tasks. The major manufacturers of big "mainframe" computers, such as IBM, took little note of the new machines—at first. But, in 1981, IBM brought out a desktop computer of its own and dubbed it the *personal computer,* or *PC.* And that started a revolution.

The PC brought computing to the people. It decentralized many office tasks. It empowered lower-level employees, greatly democratizing the workplace. And, with the rise of the Internet (see "1969: ARPANET, Precursor to the Internet, Is Activated"), the PC became a veritable window to the world, an advance in the creation and dissemination of knowledge paralleled only by the invention of printing (see "1454: Johannes Gutenberg Invents the Modern Printing Press").

Robert K. Jarvik Develops an Artificial Heart

The American physician Robert K. Jarvik did not invent the concept of an artificial pump to replace the heart—these had been tried, with little success, as early as 1969—but he did develop the first truly promising one. A "Jarvik heart" was implanted into the chest of Barney Clark on December 1, 1982. He lived 112 days with it.

The Jarvik heart was a technological wonder, which promised to free persons with irreparable heart ailments from having to wait for a suitable organ donor and heart transplant surgery, but it also made dramatically clear the limits of technological attempts to duplicate the wonders of the human body. The Jarvik heart extended life somewhat, but that life was significantly degraded in quality. Moreover, the powerful pump required an external power source, which meant that the recipient was more or less tethered for the duration of whatever life he or she had left. A handful of other patients received the Jarvik heart, but the device was soon abandoned.

Since then, some artificial-heart research has continued. The so-called AbioCor Replacement Heart, developed by Abiomed, Inc., at the beginning of the twenty-first century, is more self-contained than the Jarvik heart. On September 13, 2001, Kentuckian Tom Christerson received the AbiCor heart in a surgery performed by Drs. Laman A. Gray, Jr., and Robert D. Dowling. Christerson died, at age seventy-one on February 7, 2003, the longest-surviving artificial heart recipient.

Karl Alex Müller and Johannes Georg Bednorz Identify Ceramic Materials Capable of Superconductivity Well Above Absolute Zero

I n 1911, Kamerlingh Onnes discovered the phenomenon of the superconductivity of certain metals as temperatures approached absolute zero (see "1911: Heike Kamerlingh Onnes Discovers Superconductivity [Electrical Conductivity with Virtually No Resistance] near Absolute Zero"). The idea of superconductivity, which would enable extraordinarily efficient electronic circuits (a boon to the development of supercomputers, among many other things), was highly attractive; however, achieving and maintaining temperatures close to absolute zero is expensive, difficult, and, in everyday applications, highly impractical. Through much of the twentieth century, scientists and engineers searched for a way to achieve superconductivity at higher temperatures, such as those achievable by immersion in cheap, easily managed liquid nitrogen. All tests on metals and metal alloys failed.

Then something entirely unexpected happened. A Swiss physicist and his German colleague, Karl Alex Müller and Johannes Georg Bednorz, began experimenting with ceramics, which are not metals, but do contain mixtures of metallic oxides. To their astonishment, they found that they could attain superconductivity at 30°K—well above the near-absolute zero temperatures achievable only with costly and difficult liquid helium cooling.

The discovery ignited a flurry of experimentation, and, soon,

MÜLLER AND BEDNORZ IDENTIFY CERAMIC MATERIALS   **285**

ceramics were found that enabled superconductivity at even higher temperatures, including the range achievable by immersion in liquid nitrogen, a cheap and safe substance. Only two problems remained: one practical, the other intellectual. Ceramic substances are not easy to standardize chemically, nor are they very easy to fabricate into such traditional conductive media as wire or film. On the intellectual front, no one has yet been able to explain just *why* ceramics permit "warm superconductivity."

1988

Climatologists Identify a Global Greenhouse Effect

Carbon dioxide in the earth's atmosphere allows the passage of relatively short-wavelength radiation, but filters out longer wavelengths. That is, the CO_2 acts like the glass of a greenhouse. It admits sunlight, but traps the longer waves of heat that are radiated by the ground and other objects within the greenhouse.

Climatologists focused worldwide attention on the "greenhouse effect" of CO_2 when they identified it as the cause of the warmest weather ever recorded in 1987 and 1988. They pointed out that industrial and automotive pollution was greatly adding to the concentration of CO_2 in the atmosphere, and they called for a general reduction in CO_2 emissions—lest the temperature continue to rise, creating disastrous drought conditions and, perhaps, even melting the polar ice caps, causing devastating floods.

NASA and the European Space Agency Deploy the Hubble Space Telescope

Throughout much of the twentieth century, astronomers were engaged in a kind of telescope race, designing and building successively larger optical telescopes, culminating in the two Keck telescopes, which became operational in 1992 and 1996 atop Mauna Kea in Hawaii. Each instrument is equipped with the equivalent of a 10-meter (393-inch-diameter) reflector, making them the largest telescopes on earth.

The operative phrase here is "on earth." For no matter how large a telescope is, it will always be limited by the interposition of the earth's atmosphere, which acts like a giant screen or filter between the telescope lens and the cosmos. The ultimate means of eliminating atmospheric interference with astronomy is to get above the atmosphere, and that is just what the National Aeronautics and Space Administration (NASA), in collaboration with the European Space Agency (ESA), did with the Hubble Space Telescope (HST).

In 1990, the HST was lofted into orbit by the space shuttle *Discovery*, which deployed it from its cargo bay, setting it on an earth orbit. The HST is equipped with a 2.4-meter reflecting telescope, capable of ten times the angular resolution of the gigantic Keck telescope and approximately thirty times more sensitivity to light. At least, that was the plan. Because of a manufacturing flaw, however, the curvature of the 2.4-meter mirror was machined inaccurately by literally less than a hair, having been made too flat by one-fiftieth of the width of a human hair, an infinitesimal error nevertheless sufficient to throw the instrument out of focus. In 1993, astronauts aboard the space shuttle *Endeavour* intercepted the HST in orbit and installed a system of small corrective mirrors, which completely fixed the problem. Immediately, HST began transmitting unprecedented images of the universe, including the very first images of stars as actual bodies rather than just points of light and images of galaxies so distant that they are veritable ambassadors from the era of the origin of the universe.

The Discovery of Extrasolar Planets Is Announced

In 1983, it was observed that the star Beta Pictoris is surrounded by a disk of gas and dust. This led to speculation that planets may form—or have already formed—around the star, creating something like our own solar system. The observation led to a search for other stars that may have planets orbiting around them. The difficulty of such a search is that stars are very bright and very distant, whereas planets have no light of their own and, compared to stars, are extremely small. Looking for planets orbiting distant stars has been compared to trying to detect the light of a firefly in front of a searchlight. Rather than attempt visual identification, astronomers have used the Doppler shift phenomenon (see "1842: Christian Johann Doppler Describes the Doppler Effect, a Cornerstone of Modern Astronomy") to detect gravitational effects caused by orbiting planets. Planets orbiting a star may be expected to cause a distinctive shift in the spectrum detected from the star. In 1995, Michel Mayor and Didier Queloz of Geneva Observatory announced that they had observed such a shift in the spectrum of the star 51 Pegasi, forty-two light-years from earth. Then, in January 1996, two American astronomers, Geoffrey Marcy and Paul Butler, announced the discovery of planets orbiting the stars 70 Virginis and 47 Ursae Majoris. Like their European colleagues, they used the Doppler shift technique, but they achieved more definitive results. The star 70 Virginis is about seventy-eight light-years from earth, 47 Ursae Majoris about forty-four light-years away. Moreover, using formulas that balance the sunlight absorbed and the heat radiated, Marcy and Butler calculated the temperature of the 70 Virginis planet at about 85°C, or 185°F—compatible with the existence of liquid water and complex organic molecules. The star 70 Virginis is almost identical to our sun. It is also believed that the planet orbiting 47 Ursae Majoris may have a region in its atmosphere that allows liquid water. In both cases, the implication is that these planets may be capable of supporting life.

Since 1995, several dozen extrasolar planets have been discovered, and the list grows continually. Most scientists believe that many of these planets are capable of supporting life.

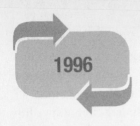

Keith Campbell, Ian Wilmut, and Others of the Roslin Institute, U.K., Clone a Sheep from the Nucleus of a Specially Cultured Cell

n 1970, recombinant DNA was developed (see "1970: Hamilton Smith and Daniel Nathans Develop Recombinant DNA, First Step Toward Genetic Engineering"), enabling DNA molecules from two or more sources to be artificially combined and then inserted into host organisms. As laboratory techniques were honed, such gene cloning could produce new genetic combinations to produce organisms with traits deemed desirable: genetically engineered bacteria to fight disease, new crops resistant to insects and parasites, or even genetically modified human beings. In 1980 and 1986, the U.S. Department of Agriculture approved the sale of the first living genetically altered organism—a virus, used as a pseudorabies vaccine—and, since then, several hundred patents have been issued for genetically altered bacteria and plants.

For the most part, this revolution in genetic engineering proceeded quietly. Then, in 1997 came the stunning news of the birth, in England, of a quite ordinary-looking lamb, named Dolly.

Ordinary-looking though she was, Dolly, unlike any other mammal in history, had no parents in the conventional sense, but was an exact duplicate of her "mother." Dolly was a clone.

Researchers had removed the nuclei from various sheep cells and implanted them into unfertilized sheep eggs, from which the natural nuclei had been removed using highly refined microsurgery techniques. This transfer gave the recipient eggs a complete set of genes, just as if the eggs had been fertilized by sperm. The eggs were cultured and then implanted into sheep. Only one of the implantations was carried to term, and the result was Dolly.

Most significant, the transferred cell nuclei did not come from embryonic cells, but from mammary cells. In other words, the cloning process did not use reproductive cells—just ordinary body cells. Traditional biology argued that no cell from any complex animal could be used to regenerate an entire organism. The successful cloning of Dolly shattered this long-held belief. However, even more shattering was the realization that a sheep, in genetic terms, is quite similar to a human being. If Dolly could be cloned, so could a human being. As had occurred on more than one occasion in the past, a great scientific advance instantly created new moral, legal, and ethical frontiers, and when Dolly developed lung disease and was euthanized on February 14, 2003, many questioned whether clones necessarily suffered health defects.

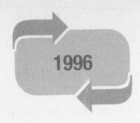

NASA Deploys *Mars Pathfinder*

Mars has long held a special place in the imagination of scientists as well as others. The most earthlike of the planets in the solar system, Mars has invited speculation that it might, like earth, harbor life. In 1906, the American astronomer Percival Lowell wrote about what he called the "canals" of Mars, thereby exciting speculation that the planet might not only support life, but intelligent life, life capable of civilization.

Well before the National Aeronautics and Space Administration (NASA) launched three important unmanned Mars probes, most scientists had stopped believing in the existence of Martian civilization, and they understood that the so-called canals were nothing more than natural formations. However, Mars continued to cry out for close exploration—and there was still the very real possibility of *some* form of life on the planet.

Mars Observer was launched on September 25, 1992, but, unfortunately, was lost on August 22, 1993. Next came *Mars Surveyor*, launched on November 7, 1996, which, after entering Mars orbit, began the long, automated process of creating a detailed low-altitude map of the Martian surface.

Mars Surveyor was a stupendous achievement, but the public was even more excited by the mission of *Mars Pathfinder*. Launched on December 4, 1996, the spacecraft landed on Mars the following summer. It employed a combination parachute and rocket-braking system, as well as an air bag system, to achieve a soft, upright landing on the Martian surface. Once it was safely landed, the spacecraft deployed a "microrover" vehicle, which traversed the area near the landing site and began transmitting some of the most extraordinary pictures human beings have ever seen. In thousands of images, ranging from broad panoramas to tight close-ups and all available to the public on a special Internet site, *Mars Pathfinder*'s microrover recorded the Martian landscape in exquisite detail.

In 1969, human beings explored a small piece of the surface of the moon (see "1969: Neil Armstrong and Edwin "Buzz" Aldrin, American Astronauts, Land on the Moon"). In 1996, using the remote-controlled microrover, *Pathfinder* did the same for a tiny patch of a planet. As for the question of life on Mars, it remains tantalizingly unresolved.

1998

The Super-Kamiokande Experiment Finds Evidence for Neutrino Mass, Providing a Clue to the Nature of 90 Percent of the Universe

Using well-established physical laws, astronomers can calculate the mass of our galaxy, the Milky Way. When they do so, they find that the visible matter in the galaxy—principally stars—accounts for only about 10 percent of its mass, perhaps even less. That is, at least 90 percent of the galaxy is invisible in the most profound sense: It does not produce nor does it reflect electromagnetic radiation at any wavelength. Extrapolating the results for the Milky Way to the universe as a whole, we must conclude that at least 90 percent of the universe likewise consists of what astronomers call "dark matter," material for which no scientist could account.

Then, in 1998, the results of the Super-Kamiokande Experiment were announced. The Super-Kamiokande Experiment uses an enormous 50,000-ton tank of highly purified water, located about 1,000 meters underground in the Kamioka Mining and Smelting Company's Mozumi Mine, Japan. This massive volume of water acts like a trap to allow study of extremely elusive neutrinos, which are created when cosmic rays, fast-moving particles from space, bombard the earth's upper atmosphere and produce cascades of secondary particles, which shower down upon the earth. Most of the neutrinos thus produced pass through the entire earth itself unscathed, undetected, and, because they were thought to be without mass, undetectable. Using the Super-Kamiokande tank, however, it is possible to image faint flashes of light given off by the neutrino interactions in the water. These flashes are detected by more than 13,000 photomultiplier tubes, which greatly amplify faint light. Using this equipment, physicists concluded that muon neutrinos oscillate, changing their type back and forth, as they travel through space or matter. Such an oscillation can occur only if the neutrino possesses mass and is not, as previously thought, massless. The Super-Kamiokande Experiment indicates that muon neutrinos oscillate into tau neutrinos, a subatomic particle that, in 1998, had yet to be detected (but see "2000: The Tau Neutrino Is Detected, Third and Last Neutrino to be Confirmed on the Standard Model of Elementary Particles").

So, what's important about discovering a neutrino with mass? As the Super-Kamiokande experimenters commented when they announced their result: "We note that massive neutrinos must now be incorporated into the theoretical models of the structure of matter and that astrophysicists concerned with finding the 'missing' or 'dark matter' in the universe must now consider the neutrino as a serious candidate." In this all-but-undetectable subatomic particle may be found 90 percent of the mass of the universe.

2000

The Human Genome Is Mapped

On April 6, 2000, Celera Genomics, a privately funded, for-profit corporation, announced that it had finished sequencing—"mapping"—the entire human genome, thereby beating the federally funded Human Genome Project, which was working toward the same goal. As the CEO of a rival firm, Neomorphic, remarked, "It's awesome. It's an incredible scientific feat. They really pushed the envelope of the technology and they've done what nobody thought could be done . . . well ahead of schedule—it's remarkable."

What had been achieved?

A "genome" contains all of the genetic material in the chromosomes of a particular organism. To sequence the human genome meant creating a map of some three billion units of DNA. With this information, it becomes possible to find a particular gene's location in the genome, to identify and find other genes in the same region, to correlate many diseases to specific genes, and to develop possible "gene therapies" to cure, prevent, or eliminate various diseases.

The genome maps resulting from both the Celera and the federally funded projects are now available to all researchers. Thus the fruits one of the greatest scientific achievements in history have been made available, worldwide, entirely free of charge.

2000

The Tau Neutrino Is Detected, Third and Last Neutrino to Be Confirmed on the Standard Model of Elementary Particles

An international consortium of fifty-four physicists working at Fermi National Accelerator Laboratory (Batavia, Illinois) announced on July 21, 2000, the first direct evidence for a subatomic particle called the tau neutrino. Past experiments had provided hints of the particle's existence, but it had never been directly observed. The tau neutrino is the third and last neutrino to be confirmed on the "standard model" of elementary particles, the most widely accepted theoretical description of the basic constituents of matter and the fundamental forces of nature. Previously discovered were the electron neutrino and the muon neutrino (see "1998: The Super-Kamiokande Experiment Finds Evidence for Neutrino Mass, Providing a Clue to the Nature of 90 Percent of the Universe"). Thus the discovery of the tau added a new dimension to an understanding of the universe at its most basic and elemental level.

The work of discovery began in 1997, when scientists used the laboratory's gigantic Tevatron accelerator to produce an intense neutrino beam, which was passed through a three-foot-thick target of iron plates sandwiched with layers of emulsion, which recorded the particle interactions. In this massive target, one out of one million million tau neutrinos interacted with an iron nucleus and transformed into a tau lepton, a particle that leaves a small (one millimeter long) track in the emulsion. That is, the tau lepton leaves tracks in the emulsion much as visible light creates an image on photographic film, but the tau does so in three dimensions. Scientists spent years sorting through approximately six million potential interactions recorded in the emulsion, until they identified a mere four events that provided convincing evidence for the tau neutrino.

2002

Scientists Grow Tadpole Eyes from Stem Cells

In April 2002, two Japanese researchers, Makoto Asashima and Ayako Sedohara of the University of Tokyo, announced that they had successfully grown—from scratch—tadpole eyeballs and had transplanted them into tadpoles. As Asashima remarked to the press, "None of the eyes were rejected and none dropped out. All of the frogs can see."

For some years prior to this, scientists had been researching stem cells as (among other things) a source of organs for transplantation. Stem cells can be cultured in the laboratory and divide for indefinite periods, giving rise to specialized cells, such as those of specific organs.

Where do these stem cells come from?

When a sperm fertilizes an egg, a single cell is created, which has the potential to form an entire organism. The fertilized egg is said to be "totipotent," its potential for development total. Within hours after fertilization, the totipotent cell divides into identical totipotent cells. About four days after fertilization and several more cell divisions, the totipotent cells start to specialize, becoming a hollow sphere of cells known as a blastocyst. From the inner cell mass of the blastocyst the tissues of the body will form. These inner cell-mass cells are called "pluripotent" because they can give rise to many types of cells, though not all types of cells necessary for fetal development. They are also called stem cells.

Some researchers have developed techniques for isolating stem cells from blastocysts—in animals as well as human beings. Others have isolated stem cells from fetal tissue obtained from terminated pregnancies. Other techniques that do not require cultivating blastocysts or using aborted embryos are also under development.

By culturing stem cells, it is possible to perform research to better understand the events that occur during human development, including the development of disease-causing problems. Stem cells are also potentially valuable for testing and developing new drugs. But most exciting of all is the possibility of generating cells and tissue for so-called cell therapies. Pluripotent stem cells may become a source of replacement cells and tissue to treat many diseases and conditions, including (for instance) Parkinson's disease, Alzheimer's disease, spinal cord injury, stroke, burns, heart disease, diabetes, osteoarthritis, and rheumatoid arthritis.

As with many scientific advances, stem cell research has met with religious and moral objections, because human embryonic tissue is involved and because some individuals believe that science has "crossed the line" into attempting to create life. At present, the stated position of the U.S. government is ambivalent. In a policy statement of August 9, 2001, President George W. Bush announced that research using existing embryonic tissue now in laboratories would be eligible for federal funding, but research involving the harvesting of new tissue would not. In Congress, competing legislative initiatives promote stem cell research or seek to limit it severely.